FROM BROKENNESS TO BLESSING: EMBRACING REDEMPTION
BY
BLAISE TSHIBWABWA

Copyright© 2024 by Blaise K. Tshibwabwa

All rights reserved. In accordance with the U.S. Copyright Act of 1976, the scanning, uploading, and electronic sharing of any part of this book without the permission of the publisher is unlawful piracy and the theft of the author's intellectual property. If you would like to use material from the book (other than for review purposes), prior written permission must be obtained by contacting the publisher at malachi.publications@gmail.com

Thank you for your support of the author's rights.

Scripture quotations are from the King James Version of the Holy Bible.

Malachi Publications
Edmonton, Alberta, Canada
Printed in Canada

Bounded in the United States of America

First paperback edition March 2024
ISBN 978-1-7779515-5-9
Illustration copyright © 2023 by Malachi Publications

Design by Malachi Publications

I thank you Lord Jesus, I thank you Holy Spirit for teaching me how to pray.

I bless your name Lord,
my Savior
and my Vindicator

Table of Contents

FOREWORD 7

PART 1 – THE JOURNEY THROUGH HOSEA 10
- *Divine Judgment* 12
- *Renewed Covenant* 17
- *Restored Love* 23
- *Spiritual Adultery* 27
- *Divine Discipline* 32
- *Repentance and Restoration* 37
- *National Rebellion* 41
- *Consequences of Idolatry* 46
- *Judgment for Israel's Idolatry* 51
- *Reaping What is Sown* 56
- *God's Unending Compassion* 61
- *Persistent Rebellion* 66
- *Consequences of Forgotten God* 71
- *Return to the Lord* 76

PART 2 – THE LORD RESPONDS TO MY CRY 81

THE CRY OF THE HEART: 85

A JOURNEY OF SEEKING GOD'S RESPONSE 85

TO OUR DEEPEST CRIES 85

THE PROMISE OF RESPONSE: 89

EMBRACING GOD'S FAITHFUL ANSWER TO OUR CRIES 89

THE CRY FOR DELIVERANCE: 93

FINDING HOPE IN GOD'S SAVING GRACE 93

THE CRY FOR HEALING: 97

EMBRACING GOD'S RESTORATIVE POWER 97

THE CRY FOR GUIDANCE: 101

TRUSTING GOD'S DIRECTION IN LIFE'S JOURNEY 101

THE CRY FOR RESTORATION: 105

FINDING HOPE IN GOD'S PROMISE OF RENEWAL 105

THE CRY OF GRATITUDE: 109

EMBRACING GOD'S ABUNDANT BLESSINGS 109

PRAYER POINTS 116

FOREWORD

In the sacred text of the Bible, the book of Hosea stands as a profound testament to the enduring love of God and the transformative power of repentance. Hosea's narrative unfolds against the backdrop of Israel's spiritual adultery and God's call to repentance, offering timeless lessons that resonate deeply with believers across generations. As we embark on this journey through the book of Hosea, we are invited to explore the depths of God's mercy, the consequences of disobedience, and the promise of redemption for those who turn back to Him.

This foreword aims to set the stage for a transformative exploration of repentance through the lens of the book of Hosea. By delving into the themes of obedience, mercy, and restoration, readers will be inspired to reflect on their own lives, embrace repentance, and experience the profound grace of God in their journey toward redemption.

In today's world, marked by spiritual turmoil and moral decay, the message of repentance proclaimed by Hosea remains as relevant as ever. From individuals wrestling with personal struggles to nations grappling with societal upheaval, the call to repentance offers a pathway to healing, reconciliation, and renewal. By examining the timeless truths of Hosea's prophecy, readers will be equipped to confront their own shortcomings, seek forgiveness, and embark on a journey of spiritual restoration.

At its core, the book of Hosea is a testament to the unfailing love of God and His relentless pursuit of His wayward children. Through the vivid imagery of Hosea's marriage to the unfaithful Gomer and the prophetic symbolism of Israel's spiritual adultery, readers are confronted with the consequences of sin and the promise of divine mercy. As we journey through the pages of Hosea, we are reminded that repentance is not merely a one-time event but a lifelong commitment to turning away from sin and turning back to God.

In conclusion, the book of Hosea serves as a powerful testament to the transformative power of repentance—a journey marked by humility, brokenness, and ultimately, restoration. As we embark on this journey together, may we be reminded of God's unfailing love and His relentless pursuit of reconciliation with His children.

May we heed the call to repentance, embrace the prodigal's path, and experience the joy of reconciliation with our Heavenly Father.

PART 1 – The Journey through Hosea

Every section begins with the actual Chapter in the Book of Hosea.

Divine Judgment

The word of the LORD that came unto Hosea, the son of Beeri, in the days of Uzziah, Jotham, Ahaz, and Hezekiah, kings of Judah, and in the days of Jeroboam the son of Joash, king of Israel.

The beginning of the word of the LORD by Hosea. And the LORD said to Hosea, Go, take unto thee a wife of whoredoms and children of whoredoms: for the land hath committed great whoredom, departing from the LORD.

So he went and took Gomer the daughter of Diblaim; which conceived, and bare him a son.

And the LORD said unto him, Call his name Jezreel; for yet a little while, and I will avenge the blood of Jezreel upon the house of Jehu, and will cause to cease the kingdom of the house of Israel.

And it shall come to pass at that day, that I will break the bow of Israel, in the valley of Jezreel.

And she conceived again, and bare a daughter. And God said unto him, Call her name Lo-Ruhamah: for I will no more have mercy upon the house of Israel; but I will utterly take them away.

But I will have mercy upon the house of Judah, and will save them by the LORD their God, and will not save them by bow, nor by sword, nor by battle, by horses, nor by horsemen.

Now when she had weaned Lo-Ruhamah, she conceived, and bare a son.

Then said God, Call his name Lo-Ammi: for ye are not my people, and I will not be your God.

Yet the number of the children of Israel shall be as the sand of the sea, which cannot be measured nor numbered; and it shall come to pass, that in the place where it was said unto them, Ye are not my people, there it shall be said unto them, Ye are the sons of the living God.

Then shall the children of Judah and the children of Israel be gathered together, and appoint themselves one head, and they shall come up out of the land: for great shall be the day of Jezreel.

-Amen.

This first chapter of the book of Hosea opens with a powerful revelation from the Lord to the prophet Hosea.

The word of the Lord comes to Hosea, instructing him to take a wife of whoredom and have children of whoredom, for the land commits great whoredom by forsaking the Lord.

This initial verse sets the stage for the overarching theme of the book—a call to repentance and restoration amidst the backdrop of spiritual adultery and unfaithfulness.

As we delve into this chapter, we encounter the symbolic significance of Hosea's marriage to Gomer, the birth of their children, and the names assigned to them by the Lord. Each aspect of this narrative serves as a poignant reminder of Israel's spiritual unfaithfulness and the consequences thereof.

Upon closer examination, we observe that Hosea's marriage to Gomer represents the covenant relationship between God and His people. Gomer's unfaithfulness mirrors Israel's spiritual adultery, as they forsake the Lord to pursue other gods and indulge in idolatry.

The birth of Hosea's children—Jezreel, Lo-Ruhamah, and Lo-Ammi—further symbolizes the judgment and consequences that await the nation due to their disobedience.

The name Jezreel, meaning "God sows," serves as a reminder of God's sovereignty and providence, even in the midst of judgment. However, it also carries connotations of punishment, as it alludes to the massacre at Jezreel prophesied by the prophet Elijah.

The names Lo-Ruhamah, meaning "No Mercy," and Lo-Ammi, meaning "Not My People," reflect the severity of God's judgment upon His people. Through these names, the Lord declares His intention to withdraw His mercy and disown His people due to their persistent rebellion and unfaithfulness.

As we apply the lessons from Hosea's prophecy to our lives today, we are confronted with the sobering reality of spiritual adultery and the consequences of forsaking the Lord. Like Israel, we are prone to wander and chase after other gods—whether they be material possessions, worldly pleasures, or selfish ambitions.

However, just as God remained faithful to Israel despite their unfaithfulness, He extends His grace and mercy to us, inviting us to repent and return to Him.

The story of Hosea and Gomer serves as a powerful metaphor for God's relentless pursuit of His people, even in the face of their rebellion and unfaithfulness. It reminds us of the depth of God's love and His desire for reconciliation with His wayward children.

Let us pray –

Heavenly Father, as we reflect on the message of Hosea's prophecy, we acknowledge our own tendency to wander and pursue other gods.

Forgive us for our spiritual adultery and unfaithfulness.

Help us to return to You wholeheartedly, to repent of our sins, and to renew our covenant relationship with You.

Thank You for Your steadfast love and unfailing mercy, which are new every morning.

May we heed Your call to repentance and experience the fullness of life found in You alone.

In Jesus' name, Amen.

Renewed Covenant

Say ye unto your brethren, Ammi; and to your sisters, Ruhamah.

Plead with your mother, plead: for she is not my wife, neither am I her husband: let her therefore put away her whoredoms out of her sight, and her adulteries from between her breasts;

Lest I strip her naked, and set her as in the day that she was born, and make her as a wilderness, and set her like a dry land, and slay her with thirst.

And I will not have mercy upon her children; for they be the children of whoredoms.

For their mother hath played the harlot: she that conceived them hath done shamefully: for she said, I will go after my lovers, that give me my bread and my water, my wool and my flax, mine oil and my drink.

Therefore, behold, I will hedge up thy way with thorns, and make a wall, that she shall not find her paths.

And she shall follow after her lovers, but she shall not overtake them; and she shall seek them, but shall not find them: then shall she say, I will go and return to my first husband; for then was it better with me than now.

For she did not know that I gave her corn, and wine, and oil, and multiplied her silver and gold, which they prepared for Baal.

Therefore will I return, and take away my corn in the time thereof, and my wine in the season thereof, and will recover my wool and my flax given to cover her nakedness.

And now will I discover her lewdness in the sight of her lovers, and none shall deliver her out of mine hand.

I will also cause all her mirth to cease, her feast days, her new moons, and her sabbaths, and all her solemn feasts.

And I will destroy her vines and her fig trees, whereof she hath said, These are my rewards that my lovers have given me: and I will make them a forest, and the beasts of the field shall eat them.

And I will visit upon her the days of Baalim, wherein she burned incense to them, and she decked herself with her earrings and her jewels, and she went after her lovers, and forgat me, saith the LORD.

Therefore, behold, I will allure her, and bring her into the wilderness, and speak comfortably unto her.

And I will give her vineyards from thence, and the valley of Achor for a door of hope: and she shall sing there, as in the days of her youth, and as in the day when she came up out of the land of Egypt.

And it shall be at that day, saith the LORD, that thou shalt call me Ishi; and shalt call me no more Baali.

For I will take away the names of Baalim out of her mouth, and they shall no more be remembered by their name.

And in that day will I make a covenant for them with the beasts of the field and with the fowls of heaven, and with the creeping things of the ground: and I will break the bow and the sword and the battle out of the earth, and will make them to lie down safely.

And I will betroth thee unto me for ever; yea, I will betroth thee unto me in righteousness, and in judgment, and in lovingkindness, and in mercies.

I will even betroth thee unto me in faithfulness: and thou shalt know the LORD.

And it shall come to pass in that day, I will hear, saith the LORD, I will hear the heavens, and they shall hear the earth;

And the earth shall hear the corn, and the wine, and the oil; and they shall hear Jezreel.

And I will sow her unto me in the earth; and I will have mercy upon her that had not obtained mercy; and I will say to them which were not my people, Thou art my people; and they shall say, Thou art my God.

-Amen.

This second chapter of the book of Hosea continues the powerful imagery and prophetic messages introduced in the first chapter.

Here, the Lord commands Hosea to plead with his brothers to plead with their mother (Israel), for she is no longer His wife, and He is no longer her husband due to her unfaithfulness. The chapter unfolds with vivid imagery of Israel's spiritual adultery, the consequences of her actions, and the promise of restoration.

As we delve into this chapter, we observe the depth of Israel's unfaithfulness and the Lord's response to her rebellion. The Lord describes Israel as an adulterous wife who pursues other lovers, symbolizing the nation's pursuit of false gods and idolatry.

Despite the Lord's blessings and provision, Israel turns away from Him, seeking fulfillment and security in worldly pleasures and alliances.

The consequences of Israel's unfaithfulness are dire, as the Lord pronounces judgment upon her. He declares that He will strip her naked, expose her shame before her lovers, and bring an end to her celebrations and festivals. The imagery of Israel's punishment serves as a stark warning of the consequences of spiritual adultery and the severity of God's judgment.

However, amidst the judgment, there is a glimmer of hope as the Lord promises to allure Israel back to Himself. He declares that He will speak tenderly to her, restore her vineyards, and renew His covenant with her. This promise of restoration demonstrates the Lord's enduring love and faithfulness, even in the face of His people's rebellion.

The message of Hosea's prophecy holds profound relevance for us today. Like Israel, we are prone to spiritual adultery, chasing after false gods and worldly pleasures instead of wholeheartedly pursuing a relationship with the Lord. However, just as the Lord pursued Israel with His love and grace, He pursues us with the same relentless affection, longing for reconciliation and restoration.

As we reflect on the consequences of Israel's unfaithfulness, we are reminded of the importance of remaining faithful to the Lord and guarding our hearts against spiritual adultery. We are called to examine our lives and identify any areas of unfaithfulness or idolatry, repenting of our sins and returning to the Lord with contrite hearts.

The promise of restoration found in this chapter fills us with hope and encouragement. It reminds us that no matter how far we may stray, the Lord is always ready and willing to forgive, restore, and renew us. His love knows no bounds, and His grace is sufficient to cover even the greatest of sins.

Let us Pray –

Heavenly Father, as we meditate on the message of Hosea's prophecy, we are humbled by Your enduring love and faithfulness towards Your people.

Forgive us for our spiritual adultery and unfaithfulness, and help us to turn wholeheartedly to You.

Thank You for Your promise of restoration and renewal, which fills us with hope and confidence in Your unfailing love.

May we remain steadfast in our commitment to You, seeking Your face and walking in Your ways all the days of our lives.

In Jesus' name, Amen.

Restored Love

Then said the LORD unto me, Go yet, love a woman beloved of her friend, yet an adulteress, according to the love of the LORD toward the children of Israel, who look to other gods, and love flagons of wine.

So I bought her to me for fifteen pieces of silver, and for an homer of barley, and an half homer of barley:

And I said unto her, Thou shalt abide for me many days; thou shalt not play the harlot, and thou shalt not be for another man: so will I also be for thee.

For the children of Israel shall abide many days without a king, and without a prince, and without a sacrifice, and without an image, and without an ephod, and without teraphim:

Afterward shall the children of Israel return, and seek the LORD their God, and David their king; and shall fear the LORD and his goodness in the latter days.

-Amen.

Here, we have a poignant illustration of the prophet's obedience to the Lord's command. Hosea is instructed to love a woman who is loved by another man, an adulteress, just as the Lord loves the Israelites despite their idolatry and unfaithfulness. This chapter serves as a continuation of the themes of redemption, restoration, and reconciliation introduced in the previous chapters.

Upon closer examination, we observe the depth of God's love and mercy as demonstrated through Hosea's actions. Despite Gomer's unfaithfulness and betrayal, Hosea chooses to love her unconditionally, mirroring the Lord's steadfast love for His people. Through Hosea's marriage to Gomer, the Lord communicates a powerful message of forgiveness, grace, and redemption.

The Lord's command to Hosea to buy back his wife from slavery further emphasizes the theme of redemption. Hosea purchases Gomer for fifteen shekels of silver and a homer and a half of barley, symbolizing the cost of redemption and the abundance of God's grace.

This act of redemption serves as a tangible representation of the Lord's desire to restore His relationship with His people, despite their waywardness and rebellion.
As we apply the lessons from Hosea's prophecy to our lives today, we are reminded of the depth of God's love and the extent of His mercy.

Like Gomer, we are prone to wander and pursue other lovers, seeking fulfillment and satisfaction in worldly pleasures and pursuits. However, just as Hosea pursued Gomer with relentless love, so too does the Lord pursue us with His unfailing grace and compassion.

The story of Hosea and Gomer serves as a powerful reminder of the redemptive power of God's love. No matter how far we may stray or how deep we may fall into sin, the Lord is always ready and willing to forgive, restore, and renew us. His love knows no bounds, and His grace is more than sufficient to cover our sins.

Let us Pray –

Heavenly Father, as we reflect on the message of Hosea's prophecy, we are humbled by Your boundless love and mercy towards Your people.

Forgive us for our waywardness and rebellion, and help us to turn back to You with contrite hearts.

Thank You for Your redemptive love, which knows no bounds and is able to restore even the most broken and wayward among us.

May we respond to Your love with gratitude and obedience, seeking to walk in Your ways and live according to Your will.

In Jesus' name, Amen.

Spiritual Adultery

Hear the word of the LORD, You children of Israel, For
the LORD *brings* a charge against the inhabitants of the land:
"There is no truth or mercy Or knowledge of God in the land.
By swearing and lying, Killing and stealing and committing
adultery, They break all restraint, With bloodshed [b]upon
bloodshed.

Therefore the land will mourn; And everyone who dwells there
will waste away With the beasts of the field And the birds of the
air; Even the fish of the sea will be taken away.

"Now let no man contend, or rebuke another; For your
people *are* like those who contend with the priest.

Therefore you shall stumble in the day; The prophet also shall
stumble with you in the night; And I will destroy your mother.

My people are destroyed for lack of knowledge. Because you
have rejected knowledge,
I also will reject you from being priest for Me; Because you have
forgotten the law of your God, I also will forget your children.

"The more they increased, The more they sinned against Me; I
will change their glory into shame.

They eat up the sin of My people; They set their [e]heart on their
iniquity.

And it shall be: like people, like priest. So I will punish them for
their ways, And reward them for their deeds.

For they shall eat, but not have enough; They shall commit harlotry, but not increase;
Because they have ceased obeying the LORD.

"Harlotry, wine, and new wine enslave the heart.

My people ask counsel from their wooden *idols,* And their staff informs them.
For the spirit of harlotry has caused *them* to stray, And they have played the harlot against their God.

They offer sacrifices on the mountaintops, And burn incense on the hills,
Under oaks, poplars, and terebinths, Because their shade *is* good.
Therefore your daughters commit harlotry, And your brides commit adultery.

"I will not punish your daughters when they commit harlotry, Nor your brides when they commit adultery; For *the men* themselves go apart with harlots, And offer sacrifices with a ritual harlot. Therefore people *who* do not understand will be trampled.

"Though you, Israel, play the harlot, Let not Judah offend. Do not come up to Gilgal,
Nor go up to Beth Aven, Nor swear an oath, *saying,* 'As the LORD lives'—

"For Israel is stubborn Like a stubborn calf; Now the LORD will let them forage Like a lamb in open country.

"Ephraim *is* joined to idols, Let him alone.

Their drink is rebellion, They commit harlotry continually. Her rulers dearly love dishonor.

The wind has wrapped her up in its wings, And they shall be ashamed because of their sacrifices.

-Amen.

Hosea, the prophet delivers a stern rebuke against the people of Israel for their spiritual adultery and rebellion against God. The chapter begins with a charge against the people, highlighting their lack of faithfulness, love, and knowledge of God.

Hosea accuses both the priests and the people of engaging in idolatry, immorality, and injustice, leading to a breakdown of society and a departure from God's ways.

As we delve into this chapter, we observe the severity of God's judgment upon His people due to their unfaithfulness. Hosea condemns the priests for their failure to uphold their responsibilities as spiritual leaders, instead leading the people astray with their idolatrous practices and corrupt behavior.

The people, in turn, are accused of exchanging the glory of God for idols, indulging in immorality, and forsaking the knowledge of God.

The consequences of Israel's rebellion are far-reaching, affecting not only their relationship with God but also their social and moral fabric. Hosea warns of the impending judgment that will befall the nation, including famine, drought, and captivity, as a result of their refusal to repent and return to the Lord.

As we apply the lessons from Hosea's prophecy to our lives today, we are confronted with the sobering reality of spiritual adultery and rebellion against God. Like the people of Israel, we are prone to wander and pursue other gods, seeking satisfaction and fulfillment in worldly pleasures and pursuits.

However, just as Hosea called the people to repentance, so too does God call us to turn away from our sins and return to Him with contrite hearts.

The message of Hosea's prophecy serves as a warning to us of the consequences of unfaithfulness and disobedience. It reminds us that God is a jealous God who will not tolerate the worship of idols or the forsaking of His commandments. Yet, amidst the judgment, there is also a message of hope and redemption, as God stands ready to forgive and restore those who turn back to Him.

Let us Pray –

Heavenly Father, as we reflect on the message of Hosea's prophecy, we are convicted of our own unfaithfulness and rebellion against You.

Forgive us for our sins and help us to turn back to You with contrite hearts.

Thank You for Your mercy and grace, which are new every morning, and for Your willingness to forgive us when we repent.

May we heed Your call to return to You and walk in Your ways, seeking to honor and glorify You in all that we do.

In Jesus' name, Amen.

31

Divine Discipline

"Hear this, O priests! Take heed, O house of Israel! Give ear, O house of the king!
For yours is the judgment, Because you have been a snare to Mizpah
And a net spread on Tabor.

The revolters are deeply involved in slaughter, Though I rebuke them all.

I know Ephraim, And Israel is not hidden from Me; For now, O Ephraim, you commit harlotry; Israel is defiled.

They do not direct their deeds toward turning to their God,
For the spirit of harlotry is in their midst, And they do not know the LORD.

The pride of Israel testifies to his face; Therefore Israel and Ephraim stumble in their iniquity; Judah also stumbles with them.

"With their flocks and herds They shall go to seek the LORD, But they will not find Him;
He has withdrawn Himself from them.

They have dealt treacherously with the LORD, For they have begotten pagan children.
Now a New Moon shall devour them and their heritage.

"Blow the ram's horn in Gibeah, The trumpet in Ramah! Cry aloud at Beth Aven, 'Look behind you, O Benjamin!'

Ephraim shall be desolate in the day of rebuke; Among the tribes of Israel I make known what is sure.

"The princes of Judah are like those who remove a landmark; I will pour out My wrath on them like water.

Ephraim is oppressed and broken in judgment, Because he willingly walked by human precept.

Therefore I will be to Ephraim like a moth, And to the house of Judah like rottenness.

"When Ephraim saw his sickness, And Judah saw his wound, Then Ephraim went to Assyria And sent to King Jareb; Yet he cannot cure you, Nor heal you of your wound.

For I will be like a lion to Ephraim, And like a young lion to the house of Judah. I, even I, will tear them and go away; I will take them away, and no one shall rescue.

I will return again to My place Till they acknowledge their offense. Then they will seek My face; In their affliction they will earnestly seek Me."

-Amen.

Judgment and warning to the people of Israel. Hosea begins by calling the priests, the house of Israel, and the house of the king to attention, declaring that judgment is imminent due to their unfaithfulness and rebellion against God. He accuses them of spiritual adultery, violence, and deceit, painting a grim picture of the consequences that await them if they do not repent and return to the Lord.

we observe Hosea's impassioned plea for the people to turn back to God before it is too late. He warns them that their unfaithfulness and rebellion have provoked the Lord's anger, resulting in punishment and destruction. The people's refusal to acknowledge their sins and seek forgiveness will only lead to further devastation and despair.

Hosea uses vivid imagery to convey the severity of God's judgment upon His people. He compares their unfaithfulness to a spreading disease and their wickedness to a rotting wound that refuses to heal.

Despite the Lord's discipline and chastisement, the people remain stubborn and unrepentant, choosing instead to seek help from Assyria and Egypt, foreign nations that will ultimately betray and destroy them.

The lessons from Hosea's prophecy to our lives today, we are confronted with the consequences of unfaithfulness and rebellion against God. Like the people of Israel, we are prone to wander and pursue other gods, seeking fulfillment and security in worldly pleasures and alliances.

However, just as Hosea called the people to repentance, so too does God call us to turn away from our sins and return to Him with contrite hearts.

The message of Hosea's prophecy serves as a sobering reminder of the importance of genuine repentance and obedience to God's commands. It warns us of the dangers of relying on human strength and worldly wisdom, rather than trusting in the Lord and seeking His guidance.

Only by turning back to God and seeking His forgiveness can we avoid the devastating consequences of spiritual adultery and rebellion.

Let us Pray –

Heavenly Father, as we reflect on the message of Hosea's prophecy, we are convicted of our own unfaithfulness and rebellion against You.

Forgive us for our sins and help us to turn back to You with contrite hearts.

Thank You for Your mercy and grace, which are new every morning, and for Your willingness to forgive us when we repent.

May we heed Your call to return to You and walk in Your ways, seeking to honor and glorify You in all that we do.

In Jesus' name, Amen.

Repentance and Restoration

Come, and let us return to the Lord; For He has torn, but He will heal us; He has stricken, but He will bind us up.

After two days He will revive us; On the third day He will raise us up, That we may live in His sight.

Let us know, Let us pursue the knowledge of the Lord. His going forth is established as the morning; He will come to us like the rain, Like the latter and former rain to the earth.

"O Ephraim, what shall I do to you? O Judah, what shall I do to you? For your faithfulness is like a morning cloud, And like the early dew it goes away.

Therefore I have hewn them by the prophets, I have slain them by the words of My mouth; And your judgments are like light that goes forth.

For I desire mercy and not sacrifice, And the knowledge of God more than burnt offerings.

"But like [d]men they transgressed the covenant; There they dealt treacherously with Me.

Gilead is a city of evildoers And defiled with blood.

As bands of robbers lie in wait for a man, So the company of priests murder on the way to Shechem; Surely they commit lewdness.

I have seen a horrible thing in the house of Israel:

There is the harlotry of Ephraim;
Israel is defiled.

Also, O Judah, a harvest is appointed for you, When I return the captives of My people.

-Amen.

Hope and Restoration amidst the backdrop of judgment and discipline. The chapter begins with a call to return to the Lord, acknowledging His sovereignty and goodness. The people express a desire to repent and seek the Lord's favor, recognizing that He is the source of healing and restoration. Hosea urges the people to press on in their pursuit of God, assuring them that He will respond to their genuine repentance with compassion and grace.

There is a contrast between the people's outward expressions of repentance and their inward condition of spiritual lukewarmness. Hosea admonishes the people for their superficial repentance, likening it to a passing cloud or morning dew that quickly fades away.

He emphasizes the importance of genuine repentance and steadfast obedience to God's commands, rather than mere ritualistic observance or empty religious practices.

Despite the people's repeated failures and shortcomings, Hosea reassures them of God's faithfulness and steadfast love. He declares that the Lord desires mercy, not sacrifice, and the knowledge of God, rather than burnt offerings.

The key to experiencing God's blessing and favor lies not in outward displays of piety, but in sincere devotion and obedience to His will. We are reminded of the importance of genuine repentance and heartfelt devotion to God. Like the people of Israel, we are prone to superficial displays of religiosity, while neglecting the weightier matters of the heart. However, God desires a relationship with us that is marked by authenticity, humility, and obedience.

The message of Hosea's prophecy challenges us to examine our own hearts and motives, ensuring that our repentance is genuine and our commitment to God is unwavering. It reminds us that God is more concerned with the condition of our hearts than with outward displays of piety or religious observance. He desires a people who will love Him wholeheartedly and walk in obedience to His commands.

Let us Pray –

Heavenly Father, as we reflect on the message of Hosea's prophecy, we are convicted of our own spiritual lukewarmness and superficiality.

Forgive us for our hypocrisy and insincerity, and help us to return to You with genuine repentance and heartfelt devotion.

Thank You for Your faithfulness and steadfast love, which endure forever.

May we seek You wholeheartedly and walk in obedience to Your will, experiencing the blessings and favor that come from a life surrendered to You.

In Jesus' name, Amen.

National Rebellion

"When I would have healed Israel, Then the iniquity of Ephraim was uncovered, And the wickedness of Samaria. For they have committed fraud; A thief comes in; A band of robbers takes spoil outside.

They do not consider in their hearts That I remember all their wickedness; Now their own deeds have surrounded them; They are before My face.

They make a king glad with their wickedness, And princes with their lies.

"They are all adulterers. Like an oven heated by a baker— He ceases stirring the fire after kneading the dough, Until it is leavened.

In the day of our king Princes have made him sick, [c]inflamed with wine; He stretched out his hand with scoffers.

They prepare their heart like an oven, While they lie in wait;
Their baker sleeps all night;
In the morning it burns like a flaming fire.

They are all hot, like an oven, And have devoured their judges; All their kings have fallen. None among them calls upon Me.

"Ephraim has mixed himself among the peoples; Ephraim is a cake unturned.

Aliens have devoured his strength, But he does not know it;

Yes, gray hairs are here and there on him, Yet he does not know it.

And the pride of Israel testifies to his face, But they do not return to the LORD their God,
Nor seek Him for all this.

"Ephraim also is like a silly dove, without sense—They call to Egypt, They go to Assyria.

Wherever they go, I will spread My net on them; I will bring them down like birds of the air; I will chastise them According to what their congregation has heard.

"Woe to them, for they have fled from Me! Destruction to them, Because they have transgressed against Me! Though I redeemed them, Yet they have spoken lies against Me.

They did not cry out to Me with their heart When they wailed upon their beds. "They assemble together for grain and new wine, They rebel against Me;

Though I disciplined and strengthened their arms, Yet they devise evil against Me;
They return, but not to the Most High; They are like a treacherous bow. Their princes shall fall by the sword For the cursings of their tongue. This shall be their derision in the land of Egypt.

-Amen.

Hosea begins by lamenting the spiritual decay and moral corruption that pervade the land, describing how the people's sins have prevented them from returning to the Lord. He highlights the prevalence of deceit, lies, and treachery among the people, as well as their refusal to acknowledge their need for repentance and restoration.

The tragic consequences of Israel's continued rebellion against God. Despite His repeated warnings and calls to repentance, the people persist in their sinful ways, forsaking the Lord and pursuing their own selfish desires. Hosea laments the nation's spiritual blindness and stubbornness, noting how their hearts are hardened against God's truth and their ears closed to His voice.

Israel's disobedience are severe, as Hosea describes how they have become like a half-baked cake, neither fully cooked nor fully risen. Their alliances with foreign nations and reliance on human strength have proven futile, leaving them vulnerable to attack and destruction. Yet, even in the midst of judgment, there is a glimmer of hope as Hosea calls the people to return to the Lord and seek His forgiveness and mercy.

Today, we are confronted with the reality of our own spiritual condition. Like Israel, we are prone to rebellion and unfaithfulness, allowing sin to separate us from God and hinder our relationship with Him. However, just as Hosea called the people to repentance, so too does God call us to turn away from our sins and return to Him with contrite hearts.

This is a reminder of God's faithfulness and steadfast love, even in the face of our disobedience and rebellion. He longs to forgive and restore us, if only we would humble ourselves, confess our sins, and seek His face. The invitation to return to the Lord is extended to each one of us, regardless of our past failures or shortcomings.

Let us Pray –

Lets the words of your Heavenly father be loud and clear in your heart, spirit and soul…

My beloved child,

I am calling out to you, inviting you to return to Me with all your heart. I have seen your struggles, your failures, and your pain, and I long to bring healing and restoration to your life. Do not allow the cares of this world or the deceitfulness of sin to harden your heart against Me. I am here, waiting with open arms, ready to forgive and to embrace you with My love and grace.

You may feel unworthy or ashamed of your past mistakes, but know that I am a God of mercy and compassion. There is nothing you have done that can separate you from My love. I have paid the price for your sins through the sacrifice of My Son, Jesus Christ, and I offer you the gift of salvation and eternal life.

Do not delay in responding to My invitation. Today is the day of salvation; now is the time to return to Me and experience the fullness of My love and grace. Repent of your sins, turn away from your waywardness, and turn to Me with a sincere and contrite heart. I will not cast you away; I will welcome you into My presence with joy and gladness.

I long to restore you, to renew you, and to transform you into the person I created you to be. Trust in Me, lean on Me, and allow Me to lead you on the path of righteousness and peace. I am with you always, guiding you, protecting you, and loving you with an everlasting love.

Come to Me, my beloved child, and let Me fill your heart with My peace, My joy, and My unfailing love. I am waiting for you with arms wide open.

Consequences of Idolatry

Set the trumpet to thy mouth. He shall come as an eagle against the house of the LORD, because they have transgressed my covenant, and trespassed against my law.

Israel shall cry unto me, My God, we know thee.

Israel hath cast off the thing that is good: the enemy shall pursue him.

They have set up kings, but not by me: they have made princes, and I knew it not: of their silver and their gold have they made them idols, that they may be cut off.

Thy calf, O Samaria, hath cast thee off; mine anger is kindled against them: how long will it be ere they attain to innocency?

For from Israel was it also: the workman made it; therefore it is not God: but the calf of Samaria shall be broken in pieces.

For they have sown the wind, and they shall reap the whirlwind: it hath no stalk; the bud shall yield no meal: if so be it yield, the strangers shall swallow it up.

Israel is swallowed up: now shall they be among the Gentiles as a vessel wherein is no pleasure.

For they are gone up to Assyria, a wild ass alone by himself: Ephraim hath hired lovers.

Yea, though they have hired among the nations, now will I gather them, and they shall sorrow a little for the burden of the king of princes.

Because Ephraim hath made many altars to sin, altars shall be unto him to sin.

I have written to him the great things of my law, but they were counted as a strange thing.

They sacrifice flesh for the sacrifices of mine offerings, and eat it; but the LORD accepteth them not; now will he remember their iniquity, and visit their sins: they shall return to Egypt.

For Israel hath forgotten his Maker, and buildeth temples; and Judah hath multiplied fenced cities: but I will send a fire upon his cities, and it shall devour the palaces thereof.

-Amen.

Israel's persistent rebellion against God. The chapter opens with Hosea proclaiming the impending judgment upon Israel for their idolatry and disobedience. He condemns the people for making alliances with foreign nations and relying on their own strength and resources rather than trusting in the Lord. Hosea warns that their idolatrous practices and reliance on human wisdom will ultimately lead to their downfall and destruction.

The depth of Israel's unfaithfulness and rebellion against God. Despite His repeated warnings and calls to repentance, the people persist in their sinful ways, seeking security and satisfaction in worldly alliances and material possessions.

Hosea laments the nation's spiritual blindness and stubbornness, noting how they have turned away from the Lord and embraced idolatry.

The consequences of Israel's disobedience are severe, as Hosea describes how they have sown the wind and will reap the whirlwind. Their pursuit of idols and reliance on human strength will only result in disappointment and destruction. Yet, even in the midst of judgment, there is a glimmer of hope as Hosea calls the people to return to the Lord and seek His forgiveness and mercy.

As we apply the lessons from Hosea's prophecy to our lives today, we are confronted with the reality of our own spiritual condition. Like Israel, we are prone to rebellion and unfaithfulness, allowing sin to separate us from God and hinder our relationship with Him.

However, just as Hosea called the people to repentance, so too does God call us to turn away from our sins and return to Him with contrite hearts.

The message of Hosea's prophecy serves as a reminder of the futility of relying on human strength and worldly wisdom. True security and satisfaction can only be found in a relationship with God, who alone is worthy of our trust and devotion. He longs to forgive and restore us, if only we would humble ourselves, confess our sins, and seek His face.

As I reflect on the message of Hosea's prophecy, I am convicted of my own tendency to rely on my own strength and understanding rather than trusting in the Lord.

How often have I pursued worldly alliances and material possessions in search of security and satisfaction, only to find myself disappointed and disillusioned?

How often have I allowed sin to separate me from God, hindering my relationship with Him and preventing me from experiencing His blessings and favor?

Yet, even in the midst of my rebellion and unfaithfulness, God remains faithful. He extends His hand of mercy and grace, inviting me to return to Him with a contrite heart. He longs to forgive and restore me, to renew me and transform me into the person He created me to be. May I heed His call to repentance, turning away from my sins and returning to Him with all my heart.

Let us Pray –

Heavenly Father, I confess my sins and shortcomings before You, knowing that You are faithful and just to forgive me and cleanse me from all unrighteousness.

Forgive me for my rebellion and unfaithfulness, for seeking security and satisfaction in worldly alliances and material possessions rather than trusting in You alone.

Help me to turn away from my sins and return to You with a contrite heart.

Fill me with Your Holy Spirit, renewing me and transforming me into the person You created me to be.

May I trust in You alone for my security and satisfaction, seeking Your will and Your ways above all else.

In Jesus' name, Amen.

Judgment for Israel's Idolatry

Rejoice not, O Israel, for joy, as other people: for thou hast gone a whoring from thy God, thou hast loved a reward upon every cornfloor.

The floor and the winepress shall not feed them, and the new wine shall fail in her.

They shall not dwell in the LORD's land; but Ephraim shall return to Egypt, and they shall eat unclean things in Assyria.

They shall not offer wine offerings to the LORD, neither shall they be pleasing unto him: their sacrifices shall be unto them as the bread of mourners; all that eat thereof shall be polluted: for their bread for their soul shall not come into the house of the LORD.

What will ye do in the solemn day, and in the day of the feast of the LORD?

For, lo, they are gone because of destruction: Egypt shall gather them up, Memphis shall bury them: the pleasant places for their silver, nettles shall possess them: thorns shall be in their tabernacles.

The days of visitation are come, the days of recompence are come; Israel shall know it: the prophet is a fool, the spiritual man is mad, for the multitude of thine iniquity, and the great hatred.

The watchman of Ephraim was with my God: but the prophet is a snare of a fowler in all his ways, and hatred in the house of his God.

They have deeply corrupted themselves, as in the days of Gibeah: therefore he will remember their iniquity, he will visit their sins.

I found Israel like grapes in the wilderness; I saw your fathers as the firstripe in the fig tree at her first time: but they went to Baalpeor, and separated themselves unto that shame; and their abominations were according as they loved.

As for Ephraim, their glory shall fly away like a bird, from the birth, and from the womb, and from the conception.

Though they bring up their children, yet will I bereave them, that there shall not be a man left: yea, woe also to them when I depart from them!

Ephraim, as I saw Tyrus, is planted in a pleasant place: but Ephraim shall bring forth his children to the murderer.

Give them, O LORD: what wilt thou give? give them a miscarrying womb and dry breasts.

All their wickedness is in Gilgal: for there I hated them: for the wickedness of their doings I will drive them out of mine house, I will love them no more: all their princes are revolters.

Ephraim is smitten, their root is dried up, they shall bear no fruit: yea, though they bring forth, yet will I slay even the beloved fruit of their womb.

My God will cast them away, because they did not hearken unto him: and they shall be wanderers among the nations.

-Amen.

Hosea prophesies about the impending judgment upon Israel for their sins, particularly their idolatry and rejection of the Lord. He describes how the people have gone astray, pursuing false gods and trusting in their own strength rather than relying on the Lord. Hosea warns that their rebellion will result in devastation and exile, as they reap the consequences of their actions.

We notice the severity of Israel's rebellion against God and the consequences they face as a result. Despite God's repeated warnings and calls to repentance, the people persist in their sinful ways, choosing to worship idols and trust in their own abilities rather than relying on the Lord. Hosea laments the nation's spiritual blindness and stubbornness, noting how they have forsaken the true God for false gods that cannot save them.

In addition to the theme of judgment and consequences, this chapter also raises the concept of the body as a temple of the Holy Spirit, as mentioned in 1 Corinthians 6:19. While the immediate context of Hosea's prophecy focuses on Israel's spiritual adultery and idolatry, the broader biblical principle of the body as a temple reminds us of the importance of honoring God with our physical bodies.

As we apply the lessons from Hosea's prophecy to our lives today, we are confronted with the reality of our own spiritual condition. Like Israel, we are prone to rebellion and unfaithfulness, allowing sin to separate us from God and hinder our relationship with Him.

However, just as Hosea called the people to repentance, so too does God call us to turn away from our sins and return to Him with contrite hearts.

The concept of the body as a temple of the Holy Spirit serves as a powerful reminder of the sacredness of our physical bodies. As followers of Christ, we are called to honor God with our bodies, treating them with respect and dignity.

This means abstaining from sexual immorality, avoiding substance abuse, and pursuing holiness and purity in all aspects of our lives.

Furthermore, just as Hosea warned Israel of the consequences of their rebellion, so too do we face consequences for our actions. When we dishonor God with our bodies through sinful behavior, we grieve the Holy Spirit and hinder our fellowship with Him.

However, when we honor God with our bodies and live in obedience to His commands, we experience the fullness of His blessings and favor.

Reflect on the message of Hosea's prophecy and the concept of the body as a temple of the Holy Spirit.

Let us Pray–

Heavenly Father, I confess my sins and shortcomings before You, knowing that You are faithful and just to forgive me and cleanse me from all unrighteousness.

Forgive me for dishonoring You with my body, for pursuing my own desires and pleasures rather than seeking to honor You in all that I do.

Help me to turn away from my sins and return to You with a contrite heart.

Fill me with Your Holy Spirit, renewing me and transforming me into the person You created me to be.

May I honor You with my body, treating it as a temple of the Holy Spirit, and may I live in obedience to Your commands all the days of my life.

In Jesus' name, Amen.

Reaping What is Sown

Israel is an empty vine, he bringeth forth fruit unto himself: according to the multitude of his fruit he hath increased the altars; according to the goodness of his land they have made goodly images.

Their heart is divided; now shall they be found faulty: he shall break down their altars, he shall spoil their images.

For now they shall say, We have no king, because we feared not the LORD; what then should a king do to us?

They have spoken words, swearing falsely in making a covenant: thus judgment springeth up as hemlock in the furrows of the field.

The inhabitants of Samaria shall fear because of the calves of Bethaven: for the people thereof shall mourn over it, and the priests thereof that rejoiced on it, for the glory thereof, because it is departed from it.

It shall be also carried unto Assyria for a present to king Jareb: Ephraim shall receive shame, and Israel shall be ashamed of his own counsel.

As for Samaria, her king is cut off as the foam upon the water.

The high places also of Aven, the sin of Israel, shall be destroyed: the thorn and the thistle shall come up on their altars; and they shall say to the mountains, Cover us; and to the hills, Fall on us.

O Israel, thou hast sinned from the days of Gibeah: there they stood: the battle in Gibeah against the children of iniquity did not overtake them.

It is in my desire that I should chastise them; and the people shall be gathered against them, when they shall bind themselves in their two furrows.

And Ephraim is as an heifer that is taught, and loveth to tread out the corn; but I passed over upon her fair neck: I will make Ephraim to ride; Judah shall plow, and Jacob shall break his clods.

Sow to yourselves in righteousness, reap in mercy; break up your fallow ground: for it is time to seek the Lord, till he come and rain righteousness upon you.

Ye have plowed wickedness, ye have reaped iniquity; ye have eaten the fruit of lies: because thou didst trust in thy way, in the multitude of thy mighty men.
Therefore shall a tumult arise among thy people, and all thy fortresses shall be spoiled, as Shalman spoiled Betharbel in the day of battle: the mother was dashed in pieces upon her children.

So shall Bethel do unto you because of your great wickedness: in a morning shall the king of Israel utterly be cut off.

-Amen

Hosea prophesies about the impending judgment upon Israel for their sins, particularly their idolatry and rejection of the Lord. He describes how the people have sown wickedness and reaped injustice, pursuing false gods and trusting in their own strength rather than relying on the Lord. Hosea warns that their rebellion will result in devastation and exile, as they reap the consequences of their actions.

Despite God's repeated warnings and calls to repentance, the people persist in their sinful ways, choosing to worship idols and trust in their own abilities rather than relying on the Lord. Hosea laments the nation's spiritual blindness and stubbornness, noting how they have forsaken the true God for false gods that cannot save them.

Hosea uses vivid agricultural imagery to illustrate the spiritual condition of Israel. He compares the nation to a luxuriant vine that once flourished under God's care but has now become degenerate and unfruitful due to their disobedience. The people have turned away from God and pursued their own desires, neglecting the covenant relationship they once shared with Him.

In addition to the theme of judgment and consequences, this chapter also highlights the concept of repentance and the importance of genuine heart transformation. Hosea urges the people to break up their unplowed ground, to seek the Lord and His righteousness, and to turn away from their sinful ways. He calls them to sow righteousness and reap the fruit of unfailing love, reminding them that only by returning to the Lord can they find true restoration and forgiveness.

As we apply the lessons from Hosea's prophecy to our lives today, we are confronted with the reality of our own spiritual condition. Like Israel, we are prone to rebellion and unfaithfulness, allowing sin to separate us from God and hinder our relationship with Him.

However, just as Hosea called the people to repentance, so too does God call us to turn away from our sins and return to Him with contrite hearts. The concept of repentance is central to the message of Hosea's prophecy. It is not enough for the people to offer superficial sacrifices or outward displays of piety; true repentance requires a genuine heart transformation.

We are called to break up the fallow ground of our hearts, to rid ourselves of the idols and sinful desires that hinder our relationship with God, and to turn back to Him with humility and sincerity.

Just as Hosea urged the people to sow righteousness and reap the fruit of unfailing love, so too are we called to live lives of holiness and obedience to God's commands. When we sow righteousness in our lives—through acts of kindness, justice, and compassion—we will reap the abundant blessings of God's unfailing love and grace.

Let us Pray –

Heavenly Father, I confess my sins and shortcomings before You, knowing that You are faithful and just to forgive me and cleanse me from all unrighteousness.

Forgive me for my rebellion and unfaithfulness, for allowing sin to take root in my life and hinder my relationship with You.

Help me to break up the fallow ground of my heart, to rid myself of the idols and sinful desires that separate me from You, and to turn back to You with humility and sincerity.

Fill me with Your Holy Spirit, renewing me and transforming me into the person You created me to be.

May I sow righteousness in my life and reap the abundant blessings of Your unfailing love and grace.

In Jesus' name, Amen.

God's Unending Compassion

"When Israel *was* a child, I loved him, And out of Egypt I called My son.

As they called them, So they went from them; They sacrificed to the Baals, And burned incense to carved images.

"I taught Ephraim to walk, Taking them by [d]their arms; But they did not know that I healed them.

I drew them with gentle cords, With bands of love, And I was to them as those who take the yoke from their neck. I stooped *and* fed them.

"He shall not return to the land of Egypt; But the Assyrian shall be his king, Because they refused to repent.

And the sword shall slash in his cities, Devour his districts, And consume *them,* Because of their own counsels.

My people are bent on backsliding from Me. Though they call to the Most High,
None at all exalt *Him.*

"How can I give you up, Ephraim? *How* can I hand you over, Israel? How can I make you like Admah? *How* can I set you like Zeboiim? My heart churns within Me; My sympathy is stirred.

I will not execute the fierceness of My anger; I will not again destroy Ephraim. For I *am* God, and not man, The Holy One in your midst; And I will not come with terror.

"They shall walk after the Lord. He will roar like a lion. When He roars, Then *His* sons shall come trembling from the west;

They shall come trembling like a bird from Egypt, Like a dove from the land of Assyria.
And I will let them dwell in their houses," Says the LORD.
"Ephraim has encircled Me with lies, And the house of Israel with deceit; But Judah still walks with God, Even with the Holy One *who is* faithful.

-Amen

God's enduring love and compassion for His people. In verse 10, Hosea proclaims, "They will follow the Lord; he will roar like a lion. When he roars, his children will come trembling from the west." This verse symbolizes the restoration and redemption that God promises to His wayward children, despite their rebellion and disobedience. It reflects the compassionate heart of God, who longs for reconciliation with His people and eagerly awaits their return to Him.

The tender portrayal of God's relationship with His people. Hosea uses vivid imagery to depict God as a loving and compassionate father, who yearns for the return of his wayward children. Despite Israel's repeated rebellion and unfaithfulness, God's love remains steadfast and unwavering. He longs to gather His people back to Himself, to restore them and shower them with His grace and mercy.

From this chapter, we also draws parallels to the creation narrative found in Genesis chapter 1, where God creates humanity in His image and declares them to be very good. From the very beginning, God has placed a high value on humanity, considering them to be His prized creation. Just as a loving parent cherishes their child, so too does God cherish His people, desiring nothing more than to see them restored to fellowship with Him.

As we apply the lessons from Hosea's prophecy to our lives today, we are reminded of the depth of God's love and compassion for us.

Despite our failings and shortcomings, God continues to pursue us with relentless love, longing for reconciliation and restoration. He calls us to return to Him, to follow Him with trembling hearts, knowing that He is eager to welcome us back into His loving embrace.

The imagery of God roaring like a lion underscores His power and authority, yet it is also a call to His children to come trembling back to Him. Just as a lion's roar can strike fear into the hearts of those who hear it, so too does God's voice command our attention and reverence. He is calling us to return to Him, to acknowledge His sovereignty and lordship over our lives, and to walk in obedience to His commands.

The parallel between Hosea 11:10 and Genesis chapter 1 serves as a powerful reminder of our intrinsic value and worth in the eyes of God. From the moment of our creation, God has considered us to be His prized possession, worthy of His love and affection. He created us to be in relationship with Him, to walk in fellowship with Him, and to experience the abundant life that He offers to all who follow Him.

Let us Pray –

Heavenly Father, thank You for Your unfailing love and compassion toward me.

Despite my failings and shortcomings, You continue to pursue me with relentless love, longing for reconciliation and restoration.

Help me to heed Your call to return to You, to follow You with trembling hearts, knowing that You are eager to welcome me back into Your loving embrace.

May I walk in obedience to Your commands, acknowledging Your sovereignty and lordship over my life.

In Jesus' name, Amen.

Persistent Rebellion

Ephraim feeds on the wind, And pursues the east wind; He daily increases lies and desolation. Also they make a covenant with the Assyrians, And oil is carried to Egypt.

"The LORD also *brings* a charge against Judah, And will punish Jacob according to his ways; According to his deeds He will recompense him.

He took his brother by the heel in the womb, And in his strength he struggled with God.

Yes, he struggled with the Angel and prevailed; He wept, and sought favor from Him.
He found Him *in* Bethel, And there He spoke to us—

That is, the LORD God of hosts. The LORD *is* His memorable name.

So you, by *the help of* your God, return; Observe mercy and justice, And wait on your God continually.

"A cunning Canaanite! Deceitful scales *are* in his hand; He loves to oppress.

And Ephraim said, 'Surely I have become rich, I have found wealth for myself;
In all my labors They shall find in me no iniquity that *is* sin.'

"But I *am* the LORD your God, Ever since the land of Egypt; I will again make you dwell in tents, As in the days of the appointed feast.

I have also spoken by the prophets, And have multiplied visions; I have given symbols through the witness of the prophets."

Though Gilead *has* idols— Surely, they are vanity— Though they sacrifice bulls in Gilgal,
Indeed their altars *shall be* heaps in the furrows of the field.

Jacob fled to the country of Syria; Israel served for a spouse,
And for a wife he tended *sheep.*

By a prophet the LORD brought Israel out of Egypt, And by a prophet he was preserved.

Ephraim provoked *Him* to anger most bitterly; Therefore his Lord will leave the guilt of his bloodshed upon him, And return his reproach upon him.

-Amen

Messages of warning and admonition to the people of Israel. He begins by recounting the history of Israel's relationship with God, highlighting their ingratitude, rebellion, and persistent disobedience. Hosea draws parallels between the patriarch Jacob and the nation of Israel, emphasizing the importance of faithfulness and obedience to God's commands.

we observe Hosea's passionate plea for the people to repent and return to the Lord. He reminds them of God's faithfulness and steadfast love throughout their history, from their humble beginnings as a nation to their present state of rebellion and apostasy. Despite God's blessings and provisions, the people continue to turn away from Him, seeking security and satisfaction in idols and foreign alliances.

Hosea warns the people of the consequences of their disobedience, urging them to turn back to the Lord before it is too late. He calls them to righteousness and justice, urging them to love mercy and walk humbly with their God. The message of Hosea's prophecy serves as a sobering reminder of the importance of faithfulness and obedience to God's commands, as well as the consequences of disobedience and rebellion. As we apply the lessons from Hosea's prophecy to our lives today, we are confronted with the reality of our own disobedience and rebellion against God.

Like the people of Israel, we are prone to wander from the path of righteousness, seeking security and satisfaction in worldly pursuits rather than trusting in the Lord. However, just as Hosea called the people to repentance, so too does God call us to turn away from our sins and return to Him with contrite hearts.

The message of Hosea's prophecy challenges us to examine our own hearts and motives, ensuring that our lives are marked by faithfulness and obedience to God's commands. It reminds us of the importance of seeking righteousness and justice, loving mercy, and walking humbly with our God.

Only by turning back to God and seeking His forgiveness can we avoid the devastating consequences of disobedience and rebellion.

Let us Pray –

Heavenly Father, as we reflect on the message of Hosea's prophecy, we are convicted of our own disobedience and rebellion against You.

Forgive us for our sins and help us to turn back to You with contrite hearts.

Thank You for Your mercy and grace, which are new every morning, and for Your willingness to forgive us when we repent.

May we heed Your call to return to You and walk in Your ways, seeking to honor and glorify You in all that we do.

In Jesus' name, Amen.

Consequences of Forgotten God

When Ephraim spoke, trembling, He exalted *himself* in Israel; But when he offended through Baal *worship*, he died.

Now they sin more and more, And have made for themselves molded images, Idols of their silver, according to their skill; All of it *is* the work of craftsmen. They say of them,

"Let the men who sacrifice kiss the calves!"

Therefore they shall be like the morning cloud And like the early dew that passes away, Like chaff blown off from a threshing floor And like smoke from a chimney.

"Yet I *am* the LORD your God Ever since the land of Egypt, And you shall know no God but Me; For *there is* no savior besides Me.

I knew you in the wilderness, In the land of [d]great drought.

When they had pasture, they were filled; They were filled and their heart was exalted; Therefore they forgot Me.

"So I will be to them like a lion; Like a leopard by the road I will lurk;

I will meet them like a bear deprived *of her cubs;* I will tear open their rib cage, And there I will devour them like a lion. The wild beast shall tear them.

"O Israel, you are destroyed, But your help *is* from Me.

I will be your King; Where *is any other,* That he may save you in all your cities? And your judges to whom you said, 'Give me a king and princes'?

I gave you a king in My anger, And took *him* away in My wrath.

"The iniquity of Ephraim *is* bound up; His sin *is* stored up.

The sorrows of a woman in childbirth shall come upon him. He *is* an unwise son, For he should not stay long where children are born.

"I will ransom them from the power of the grave; I will redeem them from death.

O Death, I will be your plagues! O Grave, I will be your destruction! Pity is hidden from My eyes."

Though he is fruitful among *his* brethren, An east wind shall come; The wind of the LORD shall come up from the wilderness. Then his spring shall become dry, And his fountain shall be dried up. He shall plunder the treasury of every desirable prize.

Samaria is held guilty, For she has rebelled against her God. They shall fall by the sword, Their infants shall be dashed in pieces, And their women with child ripped open.

-Amen

The prophet continues to deliver messages of judgment and warning to the people of Israel. Hosea begins by comparing Israel's apostasy to a worthless vine that bears no fruit, despite God's nurturing and care. He accuses the people of ingratitude and rebellion, likening them to a stubborn calf that refuses to submit to the yoke.

We observe Hosea's passionate plea for the people to repent and return to the Lord. He recounts God's faithfulness and steadfast love throughout their history, from their miraculous deliverance from Egypt to their present state of rebellion and apostasy. Despite God's blessings and provisions, the people continue to turn away from Him, seeking security and satisfaction in idols and foreign alliances.

Hosea warns the people of the consequences of their disobedience, urging them to turn back to the Lord before it is too late. He compares their fate to that of a wild beast that will be devoured by the sword, emphasizing the severity of God's judgment upon the unrepentant.

The message of Hosea's prophecy serves as a sobering reminder of the importance of faithfulness and obedience to God's commands, as well as the consequences of disobedience and rebellion.

As we apply the lessons from Hosea's prophecy to our lives today, we are confronted with the reality of our own disobedience and rebellion against God. Like the people of Israel, we are prone to wander from the path of righteousness, seeking security and satisfaction in worldly pursuits rather than trusting in the Lord.

However, just as Hosea called the people to repentance, so too does God call us to turn away from our sins and return to Him with contrite hearts.

The message of Hosea's prophecy challenges us to examine our own hearts and motives, ensuring that our lives are marked by faithfulness and obedience to God's commands. It reminds us of the importance of seeking righteousness and justice, loving mercy, and walking humbly with our God.

Only by turning back to God and seeking His forgiveness can we avoid the devastating consequences of disobedience and rebellion.

Amen

Heavenly Father, as we reflect on the message of Hosea's prophecy, we are convicted of our own disobedience and rebellion against You.

Forgive us for our sins and help us to turn back to You with contrite hearts.

Thank You for Your mercy and grace, which are new every morning, and for Your willingness to forgive us when we repent.

May we heed Your call to return to You and walk in Your ways, seeking to honor and glorify You in all that we do.

In Jesus' name, Amen.

Return to the Lord

Beloved, this is the final Chapter of Hosea and I encourage you to not only read it but to pray it.

O Israel, return to the LORD your God, For you have stumbled because of your iniquity;

Take words with you, And return to the LORD. Say to Him,

"Take away all iniquity; Receive *us* graciously, For we will offer the sacrifices of our lips.

Assyria shall not save us, We will not ride on horses, Nor will we say anymore to the work of our hands, '*You are* our gods.' For in You the fatherless finds mercy."

"I will heal their backsliding, I will love them freely, For My anger has turned away from him.

I will be like the dew to Israel; He shall grow like the lily, And lengthen his roots like Lebanon.

His branches shall spread; His beauty shall be like an olive tree, And his fragrance like Lebanon.

Those who dwell under his shadow shall return; They shall be revived *like* grain, And grow like a vine. Their scent *shall be* like the wine of Lebanon.

"Ephraim *shall say,* 'What have I to do anymore with idols?' I have heard and observed him. I *am* like a green cypress tree; Your fruit is found in Me."

Who *is* wise? Let him understand these things. *Who is* prudent? Let him know them.

For the ways of the LORD *are* right; The righteous walk in them,
But transgressors stumble in them.

-Amen

In this thirteenth chapter of the book of Hosea, the prophet continues to deliver messages of judgment and warning to the people of Israel. Hosea begins by comparing Israel's apostasy to a worthless vine that bears no fruit, despite God's nurturing and care. He accuses the people of ingratitude and rebellion, likening them to a stubborn calf that refuses to submit to the yoke.

As we delve into this chapter, we observe Hosea's passionate plea for the people to repent and return to the Lord. He recounts God's faithfulness and steadfast love throughout their history, from their miraculous deliverance from Egypt to their present state of rebellion and apostasy. Despite God's blessings and provisions, the people continue to turn away from Him, seeking security and satisfaction in idols and foreign alliances.

Hosea warns the people of the consequences of their disobedience, urging them to turn back to the Lord before it is too late. He compares their fate to that of a wild beast that will be devoured by the sword, emphasizing the severity of God's judgment upon the unrepentant.

The message of Hosea's prophecy serves as a sobering reminder of the importance of faithfulness and obedience to God's commands, as well as the consequences of disobedience and rebellion.

As we apply the lessons from Hosea's prophecy to our lives today, we are confronted with the reality of our own disobedience and rebellion against God. Like the people of Israel, we are prone to wander from the path of righteousness, seeking security and satisfaction in worldly pursuits rather than trusting in the Lord. However, just as Hosea called the people to repentance, so too does God call us to turn away from our sins and return to Him with contrite hearts.

The message of Hosea's prophecy challenges us to examine our own hearts and motives, ensuring that our lives are marked by faithfulness and obedience to God's commands. It reminds us of the importance of seeking righteousness and justice, loving mercy, and walking humbly with our God.

Only by turning back to God and seeking His forgiveness can we avoid the devastating consequences of disobedience and rebellion.

Let us Pray –

Heavenly Father, as we reflect on the message of Hosea's prophecy, we are convicted of our own disobedience and rebellion against You.

Forgive us for our sins and help us to turn back to You with contrite hearts.

Thank You for Your mercy and grace, which are new every morning, and for Your willingness to forgive us when we repent.

May we heed Your call to return to You and walk in Your ways, seeking to honor and glorify You in all that we do.

In Jesus' name, amen.

Amen.

The thirteenth chapter of Hosea's prophecy serves as a powerful reminder of the consequences of disobedience and rebellion against God.

It challenges us to examine our own lives and ensure that we are walking in faithfulness and obedience to His commands.

Let us heed the warnings of Hosea and turn back to the Lord with contrite hearts, seeking His forgiveness and mercy.

May we strive to live lives that are pleasing to God, walking in righteousness and justice, and loving mercy as we humbly walk with our God.

PART 2 – The Lord Responds to My Cry

PART 2 - The Lord Responds to My Cry

In the depths of our despair, when it feels like all hope is lost, we cry out to the Lord, seeking His presence, His comfort, and His guidance. This Part is a testament to the faithfulness of God in responding to our cries and leading us into a deeper relationship with Him.

Through stories, scriptures, and prayers, we will explore how the Lord responds to our cries with compassion, mercy, and grace, transforming our lives and restoring our souls.

The Cry of the Heart:

A Journey of Seeking God's Response to Our Deepest Cries

In the silence of the night, in the depths of our solitude, there is a cry that echoes within us—a cry of the heart. It is a cry that transcends language, a primal expression of our deepest longings, fears, and desires. In this chapter, we embark on a journey into the depths of the human heart, exploring the significance of our cries before the Lord and His faithful response to each one.

The human heart is a complex and mysterious realm, filled with a myriad of emotions, desires, and vulnerabilities. It is a place where joy and sorrow, hope and despair, love and longing intertwine, creating a symphony of emotions that reverberates throughout our being. At times, our hearts overflow with gratitude and praise, while at other times, they are weighed down by the burdens of life, echoing with cries of pain and anguish.

Cries of Pain and Anguish:

We cannot escape the reality of suffering in this fallen world. From physical ailments to emotional wounds, from broken relationships to shattered dreams, we experience pain and anguish in various forms. In the depths of our despair, we cry out to the Lord, pouring out our hearts before Him, seeking solace and comfort in His presence. It is in these moments of vulnerability that we discover the depth of God's compassion and mercy, as He draws near to the brokenhearted and binds up their wounds.

Cries of Longing and Desperation:

In the midst of life's trials and tribulations, we long for something more—something beyond the transient pleasures of this world. Our hearts yearn for meaning and purpose, for love and acceptance, for fulfillment and joy. Yet, in our search for significance, we often find ourselves wandering in the wilderness, feeling lost and alone. It is in these moments of desperation that we cry out to the Lord, seeking His guidance and direction, His peace and provision. And though the road may be long and the journey difficult, we trust in His promise to lead us beside still waters and restore our souls.

The Significance of Our Cries Before the Lord.

Our cries before the Lord are not mere words spoken into the void; they are sacred utterances that pierce the heavens and reach the very throne of God. They are the language of the soul, the cry of the heart that transcends earthly limitations and touches the heart of the Almighty. In our cries, God hears the longing of our hearts, the pain of our sorrows, the desperation of our prayers. And though we may not always understand His ways or His timing, we trust in His promise to never leave us nor forsake us, to be our refuge and strength in times of trouble.

God's Response to Our Cries:

The beauty of our cries before the Lord lies not in our eloquence or our righteousness, but in His unfailing love and faithfulness. For He is a God who hears the cries of His people and responds with compassion and grace. He is the God who draws near to the brokenhearted and binds up their wounds, who comforts us in our affliction and sustains us in our distress. He is the God who turns our mourning into dancing, who brings beauty from ashes and joy from sorrow.

The Promise of Response:

Embracing God's Faithful Answer to Our Cries

In the journey of faith, there is a profound assurance that accompanies our cries before the Lord—the promise of response. In this chapter, we delve into the scriptures to explore the unwavering faithfulness of God in hearing and responding to our cries, drawing comfort and strength from His enduring promises.

The Foundation of God's Promise:

At the heart of the Christian faith lies the foundational truth that God is a God who hears and answers prayers. Throughout the pages of Scripture, we see evidence of His faithfulness in responding to the cries of His people, from the cries of the Israelites in Egypt to the prayers of the prophets and apostles.

In *Psalm 34:17-18*, we read, "The righteous cry out, and the Lord hears them; he delivers them from all their troubles. The Lord is close to the brokenhearted and saves those who are crushed in spirit." This passage serves as a poignant reminder of God's promise to respond to the cries of His people with compassion and deliverance.

The Cry of the Righteous:

As believers, we are called to live lives of righteousness and obedience to God's word. In *1 John 5:14-15*, we are assured, "This is the confidence we have in approaching God: that if we ask anything according to his will, he hears us. And if we know that he hears us—whatever we ask—we know that we have what we asked of him." This passage underscores the importance of aligning our prayers with God's will and trusting in His promise to hear and answer us according to His perfect plan.

The Cry of the Brokenhearted:

In times of trial and tribulation, our hearts cry out to God for comfort and deliverance. In *Isaiah 65:24*, we find assurance in God's promise to respond to the cries of His people, "Before they call I will answer; while they are still speaking I will hear." This verse serves as a powerful reminder that God is not only aware of our needs before we even articulate them, but He is also eager to respond to our cries with compassion and grace.

The Cry of the Faithful:

Throughout the Bible, we see examples of God's faithful response to the cries of His faithful servants. In *2 Chronicles 7:14*, God promises, "If my people, who are called by my name, will humble themselves and pray and seek my face and turn from their wicked ways, then I will hear from heaven, and I will forgive their sin and will heal their land." This passage emphasizes the importance of repentance and seeking God's face in prayer, knowing that He is faithful to respond with forgiveness and healing.

The Cry of the Needy:

In *Psalm 107:19-20*, we find comfort in God's promise to respond to the cries of the needy, "Then they cried to the Lord in their trouble, and he saved them from their distress. He sent out his word and healed them; he rescued them from the grave." This passage serves as a powerful reminder that God is a God of mercy and compassion, who responds to the cries of the needy with salvation and deliverance.

The promise of response is a central theme in the Christian faith, rooted in the unwavering faithfulness of God. As we journey through life's trials and tribulations, may we take comfort in knowing that our cries before the Lord are not in vain, but are met with His compassionate response. May we continue to trust in His promises, knowing that He hears our cries and is faithful to deliver us according to His perfect will. Amen.

The Cry for Deliverance: Finding Hope in God's Saving Grace

In the depths of despair, when we feel overwhelmed by the trials of life, there is a cry that rises from the depths of our souls—a cry for deliverance. In this chapter, we delve into the scriptures to explore the cry for deliverance, finding hope and assurance in God's saving grace.

The Cry of the Israelites:

The cry for deliverance is a recurring theme throughout the Bible, beginning with the cry of the Israelites in Egypt. In *Exodus 2:23-25*, we read, "During that long period, the king of Egypt died. The Israelites groaned in their slavery and cried out, and their cry for help because of their slavery went up to God. God heard their groaning and he remembered his covenant with Abraham, with Isaac and with Jacob. So God looked on the Israelites and was concerned about them." This passage serves as a powerful reminder that God is attentive to the cries of His people and is faithful to deliver them from bondage.

The Cry of the Psalmist:

Throughout the Psalms, we see examples of the cry for deliverance expressed by the Psalmist. In *Psalm 40:1-3*, David writes, "I waited patiently for the Lord; he turned to me and heard my cry. He lifted me out of the slimy pit, out of the mud and mire; he set my feet on a rock and gave me a firm place to stand. He put a new song in my mouth, a hymn of praise to our God. Many will see and fear the Lord and put their trust in him." This passage serves as a testimony to God's faithfulness in delivering His people from the depths of despair and setting their feet on solid ground.

The Cry of Jonah:

In the book of Jonah, we see the cry for deliverance expressed by the prophet Jonah as he finds himself in the belly of a great fish. In *Jonah 2:1-2*, Jonah cries out to the Lord, saying, "In my distress I called to the Lord, and he answered me. From deep in the realm of the dead I called for help, and you listened to my cry." This passage serves as a powerful reminder that even in the most desperate of circumstances, God is able to hear and answer our cries for deliverance.

The Cry of Jesus:

Even Jesus Himself experienced the cry for deliverance in the garden of Gethsemane, as He faced the agony of the cross. In *Matthew 26:39*, Jesus prays, "My Father, if it is possible, may this cup be taken from me. Yet not as I will, but as you will." This passage serves as a poignant reminder that even the Son of God cried out to the Father in His hour of need, trusting in His sovereign will and ultimate deliverance.

The Cry for Spiritual Deliverance:

In addition to physical deliverance, we also cry out to God for spiritual deliverance from the bondage of sin and death. In *Romans 7:24-25*, the apostle Paul writes, "What a wretched man I am! Who will rescue me from this body that is subject to death? Thanks be to God, who delivers me through Jesus Christ our Lord!" This passage serves as a powerful reminder that our ultimate deliverance comes through Jesus Christ, who has conquered sin and death through His death and resurrection.

The cry for deliverance is a universal cry that echoes throughout the pages of Scripture and resonates within the hearts of believers today. Whether facing physical trials or spiritual bondage, we can take comfort in knowing that God hears our cries for deliverance and is faithful to answer according to His perfect will. May we continue to cry out to the Lord in our times of need, trusting in His saving grace to deliver us from all that seeks to ensnare us. Amen.

The Cry for Healing:
Embracing God's Restorative Power

In the midst of pain and suffering, there is a cry that echoes from the depths of our souls—a cry for healing. In this chapter, we explore the cry for healing as expressed throughout the Bible, drawing comfort and hope from God's promises of restoration and wholeness.

The Cry of the Afflicted:

From physical ailments to emotional wounds, the cry for healing is a universal expression of human suffering. In *Psalm 30:2*, the Psalmist declares, "Lord my God, I called to you for help, and you healed me." This passage serves as a powerful reminder that God is attentive to the cries of the afflicted and is able to bring healing and restoration to all who call upon His name.

The Healing Ministry of Jesus:

Throughout the New Testament, we see Jesus demonstrating His power and authority to heal the sick and afflicted. In *Matthew 4:23-24*, we read, "Jesus went throughout Galilee, teaching in their synagogues, proclaiming the good news of the kingdom, and healing every disease and sickness among the people. News about him spread all over Syria, and people brought to him all who were ill with various diseases, those suffering severe pain, the demon-possessed, those having seizures, and the paralyzed; and he healed them." This passage serves as a testament to Jesus' compassionate ministry of healing, demonstrating God's desire to bring wholeness and restoration to His people.

The Cry for Spiritual Healing:

In addition to physical healing, we also cry out to God for spiritual healing from the wounds of sin and brokenness. In *Isaiah 53:5*, the prophet declares, "But he was pierced for our transgressions, he was crushed for our iniquities; the punishment that brought us peace was on him, and by his wounds we are healed." This passage serves as a powerful reminder that Jesus' sacrificial death on the cross not only provides forgiveness for our sins but also brings healing and restoration to our souls.

The Cry for Emotional Healing:

In times of emotional pain and distress, we cry out to God for healing and comfort. In *Psalm 147:3*, the Psalmist writes, "He heals the brokenhearted and binds up their wounds." This passage serves as a source of comfort and assurance, reminding us that God is near to the brokenhearted and is able to bring healing and restoration to the deepest wounds of our souls.

The Cry for Intercessory Healing:

As members of the body of Christ, we are called to pray for one another and to lift up those who are in need of healing. In *James 5:14-15*, we are instructed, "Is anyone among you sick? Let them call the elders of the church to pray over them and anoint them with oil in the name of the Lord. And the prayer offered in faith will make the sick person well; the Lord will raise them up. If they have sinned, they will be forgiven." This passage serves as a reminder of the power of intercessory prayer in bringing healing and restoration to those who are in need.

The cry for healing is a powerful expression of human suffering, but it is also a testament to God's compassion and grace.

Whether facing physical, emotional, or spiritual affliction, we can take comfort in knowing that God hears our cries for healing and is faithful to respond with His restorative power.

May we continue to cry out to the Lord in our times of need, trusting in His promise to bring healing and wholeness to all who call upon His name. Amen.

The Cry for Guidance:

Trusting God's Direction in Life's Journey

In the journey of life, there are moments when we find ourselves at a crossroads, uncertain of which path to take. It is in these moments that we cry out to God for guidance, seeking His wisdom and direction to navigate the complexities of life. In this chapter, we delve into the cry for guidance, exploring how God's word provides us with clarity and assurance as we trust in His leading.

The Cry for Guidance in Scripture:

Throughout the Bible, we see examples of individuals crying out to God for guidance in their lives. In *Psalm 25:4-5*, the Psalmist writes, "Show me your ways, Lord, teach me your paths. Guide me in your truth and teach me, for you are God my Savior, and my hope is in you all day long." This passage serves as a powerful reminder of the importance of seeking God's guidance in every aspect of our lives, trusting in His wisdom and understanding.

The Promise of God's Guidance:

God has promised to guide and direct His people in the paths of righteousness. In *Proverbs 3:5-6*, we read, "Trust in the Lord with all your heart and lean not on your own understanding; in all your ways submit to him, and he will make your paths straight." This passage serves as a comforting assurance that as we trust in the Lord and seek His guidance, He will lead us on the right path and make our way clear.

The Guidance of the Holy Spirit:

In addition to seeking guidance through prayer and meditation on God's word, we are also blessed with the guidance of the Holy Spirit. In *John 16:13*, Jesus promises, "But when he, the Spirit of truth, comes, he will guide you into all the truth. He will not speak on his own; he will speak only what he hears, and he will tell you what is yet to come." This passage serves as a reminder of the indwelling presence of the Holy Spirit in our lives, guiding us into all truth and leading us in the ways of righteousness.

The Example of Jesus:

As followers of Christ, we look to Jesus as our ultimate example of obedience and trust in God's guidance. In *John 5:19*, Jesus declares, "Very truly I tell you, the Son can do nothing by himself; he can do only what he sees his Father doing, because whatever the Father does the Son also does." This passage serves as a model for us to follow, as we seek to align our will with the will of the Father and trust in His guidance for our lives.

Trusting God's Timing:

In our cry for guidance, it is important to remember that God's timing is perfect. In *Isaiah 55:8-9*, we read, "For my thoughts are not your thoughts, neither are your ways my ways," declares the Lord. "As the heavens are higher than the earth, so are my ways higher than your ways and my thoughts than your thoughts." This passage serves as a reminder that God's ways are beyond our understanding, and we must trust in His timing and His plans, knowing that He works all things together for our good.

The cry for guidance is a natural expression of our dependence on God's wisdom and understanding in navigating the complexities of life. As we seek His guidance through prayer, meditation on His word, and the leading of the Holy Spirit, may we trust in His faithfulness to lead us on the right path and make our way clear.

May we follow the example of Jesus in obedience and trust, knowing that His plans for us are good, and His timing is perfect. Amen.

The Cry for Restoration:

Finding Hope in God's Promise of Renewal

In the brokenness of life, there is a cry that rises from the depths of our souls—a cry for restoration. In this chapter, we explore the cry for restoration as expressed throughout the Bible, drawing comfort and strength from God's promises of renewal and redemption.

The Cry for Restoration in Scripture:

Throughout the pages of Scripture, we see examples of individuals and communities crying out to God for restoration in times of distress and despair. In *Joel 2:25-26*, the prophet declares, "I will repay you for the years the locusts have eaten—the great locust and the young locust, the other locusts and the locust swarm—my great army that I sent among you. You will have plenty to eat, until you are full, and you will praise the name of the Lord your God, who has worked wonders for you; never again will my people be shamed." This passage serves as a powerful reminder of God's promise to restore what has been lost and to bring abundance and blessing to His people.

The Promise of Restoration:

God has promised to restore His people and to bring renewal to all areas of their lives. In *Isaiah 61:1-3*, we read, "The Spirit of the Sovereign Lord is on me, because the Lord has anointed me to proclaim good news to the poor. He has sent me to bind up the brokenhearted, to proclaim freedom for the captives and release from darkness for the prisoners, to proclaim the year of the Lord's favor and the day of vengeance of our God, to comfort all who mourn, and provide for those who grieve in Zion—to bestow on them a crown of beauty instead of ashes, the oil of joy instead of mourning, and a garment of praise instead of a spirit of despair. They will be called oaks of righteousness, a planting of the Lord for the display of his splendor." This passage serves as a powerful declaration of God's intention to bring restoration and renewal to His people, transforming their mourning into joy and their despair into praise.

The Restoration of Relationships:

One of the most profound aspects of God's restoration is the healing of broken relationships. In *Colossians 3:12-14*, the apostle Paul writes, "Therefore, as God's chosen people, holy and dearly loved, clothe yourselves with compassion, kindness, humility, gentleness and patience. Bear with each other and forgive one another if any of you has a grievance against someone. Forgive as the Lord forgave you. And over all these virtues put on love, which binds them all together in perfect unity." This passage serves as a reminder that God's restoration extends to our relationships with one another, as we forgive one another and strive for unity in love.

The Cry for Spiritual Restoration:

In addition to physical and relational restoration, we also cry out to God for spiritual renewal and transformation. In *Psalm 51:10-12*, King David cries out to God, saying, "Create in me a pure heart, O God, and renew a steadfast spirit within me. Do not cast me from your presence or take your Holy Spirit from me. Restore to me the joy of your salvation and grant me a willing spirit, to sustain me." This passage serves as a heartfelt plea for God to renew and restore David's spiritual life, bringing him back into intimate fellowship with the Lord.

The Ultimate Restoration in Christ:

Ultimately, our cry for restoration finds its fulfillment in Jesus Christ, who came to bring redemption and renewal to all who believe in Him. In *Revelation 21:5*, we read, "He who was seated on the throne said, 'I am making everything new!' Then he said, 'Write this down, for these words are trustworthy and true.'" This passage serves as a powerful declaration of God's ultimate plan to restore all things in Christ, bringing an end to sin, suffering, and death, and ushering in a new heaven and a new earth where righteousness dwells.

The cry for restoration is a profound expression of our longing for renewal and redemption in the midst of life's brokenness. As we cry out to God for restoration, may we take comfort in His promises of renewal and redemption, trusting in His faithfulness to bring healing and wholeness to every area of our lives. May we find hope and strength in Jesus Christ, who is our ultimate source of restoration and renewal. Amen.

The Cry of Gratitude:
Embracing God's Abundant Blessings

In the journey of faith, there is a cry that rises from the depths of our souls—a cry of gratitude. In this chapter, we explore the cry of gratitude as a response to God's abundant blessings, drawing inspiration from Scripture and personal testimonies of thanksgiving.

The Biblical Foundation of Gratitude:

Gratitude is a central theme throughout the Bible, woven into the fabric of God's relationship with His people. In *Psalm 107:1*, the Psalmist declares, "Give thanks to the Lord, for he is good; his love endures forever." This passage serves as a powerful reminder of the importance of expressing gratitude to God for His goodness and steadfast love.

The Example of Jesus:

Jesus Himself modeled a life of gratitude, giving thanks to God in all circumstances. In *Matthew 15:36*, we read, "Then he took the seven loaves and the fish, and when he had given thanks, he broke them and gave them to the disciples, and they in turn to the people." This passage serves as a reminder that even in times of scarcity, Jesus gave thanks to God for His provision, setting an example for us to follow in expressing gratitude in all circumstances.

The Call to Thankfulness:

Throughout the New Testament, believers are encouraged to cultivate a spirit of thankfulness in their lives. In *Colossians 3:17*, the apostle Paul writes, "And whatever you do, whether in word or deed, do it all in the name of the Lord Jesus, giving thanks to God the Father through him." This passage serves as a reminder that thankfulness should permeate every aspect of our lives, as we acknowledge God's sovereignty and provision in all things.

The Power of Gratitude:

Gratitude has the power to transform our hearts and minds, leading to a deeper sense of joy and contentment. In *Philippians 4:6-7*, the apostle Paul writes, "Do not be anxious about anything, but in every situation, by prayer and petition, with thanksgiving, present your requests to God. And the peace of God, which transcends all understanding, will guard your hearts and your minds in Christ Jesus." This passage serves as a reminder that thanksgiving leads to peace, as we trust in God's provision and care for us.

The Cry of Gratitude in Worship:

One of the most powerful expressions of gratitude is found in the context of worship. In *Psalm 100:4-5*, the Psalmist writes, "Enter his gates with thanksgiving and his courts with praise; give thanks to him and praise his name. For the Lord is good and his love endures forever; his faithfulness continues through all generations." This passage serves as a reminder that gratitude should be a central aspect of our worship, as we lift our voices in praise and thanksgiving to God for His goodness and faithfulness.

The Fruit of Gratitude:

Gratitude is not only a response to God's blessings but also a catalyst for further blessings in our lives. In *Luke 17:11-19*, we read the story of Jesus healing ten lepers, and only one returning to give thanks. Jesus responds, "Were not all ten cleansed? Where are the other nine? Has no one returned to give praise to God except this foreigner?"

This passage serves as a reminder that gratitude opens the door to deeper intimacy with God and further blessings in our lives.

The cry of gratitude is a powerful expression of our recognition of God's goodness and provision in our lives. As we cultivate a spirit of thankfulness, may we be reminded of God's faithfulness and love for us, leading to a deeper sense of joy and contentment. May our lives be marked by a continual cry of gratitude, as we give thanks to God for His abundant blessings. Amen.

Let us pause and reflect on the faithfulness of God in responding to our cries. Throughout the preceding chapters, we have explored various aspects of the Christian faith— from seeking guidance to experiencing restoration, from crying out for healing to embracing gratitude. In each chapter, we have seen how God hears our cries and responds with compassion and love. let us be reminded of God's goodness and grace, and let our hearts be filled with gratitude and praise as we journey forward in faith.

One of the central themes of the Christian faith is the belief in God's faithfulness in responding to our cries. Throughout the Bible, we see countless examples of individuals and communities crying out to God in times of need, and God responding with compassion and grace. From the Israelites crying out for deliverance from slavery in Egypt to the disciples crying out for help in the midst of a storm at sea, we see how God hears our cries and responds with power and love.

In Psalm *34:17-18*, we read, "The righteous cry out, and the Lord hears them; he delivers them from all their troubles. The Lord is close to the brokenhearted and saves those who are crushed in spirit." This passage serves as a powerful reminder of God's faithfulness in responding to the cries of His people. No matter how desperate or hopeless our situation may seem, we can take comfort in knowing that God hears our cries and is near to those who are brokenhearted.

As we reflect on God's faithfulness in responding to our cries, we are called to trust in His goodness and grace. In *Psalm 100:5*, the Psalmist declares, "For the Lord is good and his love endures forever; his faithfulness continues through all generations." This passage serves as a reminder that God is good and His love for us is eternal. Even when we cannot see the outcome of our circumstances, we can trust that God is working all things together for our good (*Romans 8:28*).

In addition to trusting in God's goodness, we are called to trust in His providence— His sovereign control over all things. In *Proverbs 3:5-6*, we read, "Trust in the Lord with all your heart and lean not on your own understanding; in all your ways submit to him, and he will make your paths straight." This passage serves as a reminder that God is in control of our lives and is able to guide us in the right direction. Even when we cannot see the way forward, we can trust that God is leading us and will make our paths straight.

As we journey forward in faith, we are called to trust in God's timing. In *Ecclesiastes 3:11*, we read, "He has made everything beautiful in its time." This passage serves as a reminder that God has a perfect plan and timing for our lives. Even when we are tempted to become impatient or discouraged, we can trust that God is working behind the scenes, orchestrating events according to His perfect will.

In response to God's faithfulness and goodness, we are called to express gratitude and praise. In *Psalm 118:1*, the Psalmist declares, "Give thanks to the Lord, for he is good; his love endures forever." This passage serves as a reminder that gratitude and praise should flow from our hearts as we reflect on God's faithfulness and grace in our lives. Whether in times of joy or sorrow, we can always find reasons to give thanks to God for His unfailing love and mercy.

let us take a moment to offer a prayer of gratitude and praise to our Heavenly Father:

Heavenly Father,
We thank you for your faithfulness and goodness in responding to our cries. You are a God who hears our prayers and answers with compassion and love. Help us to trust in your providence and timing, knowing that you are working all things together for our good. Fill our hearts with gratitude and praise as we journey

forward in faith, knowing that you are with us every step of the way. Amen.

May we be reminded of the faithfulness of God in responding to our cries. Let us continue to trust in His goodness and grace, knowing that He hears our cries and responds with compassion and love. May our hearts be filled with gratitude and praise as we journey forward in faith, knowing that the Lord is with us always. Amen.

PRAYER POINTS

Thank God for His mighty power to save and for the power of deliverance form any form of bondage.

Heavenly Father, we thank You for the word delivered through Your servant Hosea, a message that transcends time and speaks to us even today. Grant us the wisdom to heed Your words as they were given in the days of Uzziah, Jotham, Ahaz, Hezekiah, and Jeroboam, that we may understand Your will for us in our time.

Lord, as You instructed Hosea to take a wife of whoredoms, symbolizing the unfaithfulness of Your people, we recognize the depths of our own sins and the ways we have strayed from You. Forgive us, O God, for our transgressions and lead us back to Your loving embrace.

Lord, as You named Jezreel to symbolize the impending judgment upon Israel, we humbly acknowledge the consequences of our actions. May Your mercy prevail even in the face of our disobedience, and may we turn to You in repentance before it is too late.

Lord, as You named Loruhamah, signifying the withdrawal of Your mercy from Israel, we beseech You to restore Your grace upon us. Though we may deserve Your judgment, in Your compassion, withhold Your wrath and shower us once again with Your unfailing love.

Lord, as You promise that the children of Israel will be as numerous as the sand of the sea, we admire at Your abundant grace and mercy. Help us to live as Your chosen people, proclaiming Your goodness to the ends of the earth.

Father, in Your mercy, spare us from the consequences of our disobedience. Prevent us from being stripped naked and left desolate, but instead, clothe us with Your righteousness and lead us beside still waters.

Heavenly Father, forgive us for seeking satisfaction in worldly pleasures and pursuits. Help us to turn away from false idols and to find our fulfillment solely in You, the source of all our needs.

Lord, in Your sovereignty, expose our sins before us and the world, that we may see the folly of our ways and turn back to You for forgiveness and restoration.

Heavenly Father, forgive us for our spiritual adultery and idolatry. May we never forget Your faithfulness and steadfast love, and may we always remain devoted to You.

Heavenly Father, remove the names of false gods from our lips, that we may worship You alone with all reverence and adoration. Let us never again stray after the idols of this world.

Lord, as the earth responds to Your commands, may we also heed Your word and obey Your will. Let our lives bear witness to Your sovereignty and majesty.

Father, sow us into the earth as a people who have obtained Your mercy and favor. Let us declare with joy and thanksgiving that You are our God, and we are Your people.

Lord, as Hosea bought the woman for fifteen pieces of silver and barley, symbolizing the redemption and restoration of Your people, we pray for the price of Your sacrifice to be evident in our lives. Help us to value the precious gift of salvation bought with the blood of Jesus Christ, and may we live as redeemed and transformed children of God, in the name of Jesus.

Father, just as You instructed Hosea's wife to abide for many days without playing the harlot or being for another man, establish in us a steadfast commitment to You. Keep us away from spiritual adultery and unfaithfulness, that we may be wholly devoted to You alone, in the name of Jesus.

I declare that I am redeemed and restored, just as Hosea bought the woman for fifteen pieces of silver and barley. The price of my redemption is evident, for I am bought with the precious blood of Jesus Christ, in the name of Jesus.

According to the word of the Lord, I am called to abide in faithfulness for many days, abstaining from spiritual harlotry and unfaithfulness. I am committed to the Lord alone, and He shall also be for me, in the name of Jesus.

declare that though there may be seasons of barrenness and lack, as foretold for the children of Israel, I remain steadfast in my trust in the Lord. Even without a visible king, prince, sacrifice, or image, I stand firm in my faith, knowing that my God is with me, in the name of Jesus.

I proclaim that the time of return and restoration is upon us, just as Hosea prophesied for the children of Israel. We shall seek the Lord our God and David our king, and we shall fear the Lord and His goodness in the latter days, in the name of Jesus. Amen.

Lord, forgive us for our sins of swearing, lying, killing, stealing, and adultery. Our transgressions have led to bloodshed and brokenness in the land. Grant us Your mercy and grace to turn away from these wicked deeds and seek Your righteousness.

Lord, may there be no contention or strife among Your people. Help us to live in harmony and unity, refraining from quarrels and disputes. Let us seek peace and reconciliation with one another, reflecting Your love and grace.

Lord, we repent for our lack of knowledge and understanding of Your ways. Forgive us for rejecting Your truth and forsaking Your commandments. Restore to us the wisdom and discernment that comes from Your Spirit.

Lord, deliver us from the bondage of sin. We renounce all iniquity and ask for Your strength to overcome temptation. May our hearts be set on righteousness and purity, aligning with Your will and purposes.

Lord, we repent for our insatiable desires and pursuit of worldly pleasures. Our hearts have turned away from You, resulting in emptiness and dissatisfaction. Restore to us the joy of Your salvation and satisfaction found only in You.

Lord, we renounce seeking counsel from idols and false gods. Help us to seek wisdom and guidance from You, the one true God. May we trust in Your leading and rely on Your word for direction in our lives.

Father, forgive us for our idolatrous practices and false worship. We repent for offering sacrifices to other gods on mountaintops and hills. Help us to worship You in spirit and in truth, honoring You alone.

Lord, cleanse me from all impurity and sin. Let my heart be purified by Your holy fire, and may my love for You burn brightly.

Remove the sourness from my drink and fill me with the sweetness of Your Spirit.

Heavenly Father, break the chains that bind us and set us free from the bondage of sin. Let Your wind of revival blow upon us, bringing healing and restoration. May we no longer be ashamed of our sacrifices but offer them with pure hearts and sincere devotion.

: Hear me, O Lord, as I come before You in prayer. Open my ears to listen to Your voice and my heart to receive Your guidance. Help me to heed Your warnings and instructions, for judgment is near. In the name of Jesus, I declare that I am attentive to the word of the Lord.

Lord, reveal to me any areas of my life where I have been ensnared by sin or where I have become a stumbling block to others. Grant me the humility to repent and turn away from all forms of rebellion and disobedience. Help me to walk in righteousness and integrity before You.

Heavenly Father, I acknowledge that You see all things, and nothing is hidden from Your sight. Forgive me for any hidden sins or secret transgressions. Cleanse me from all unrighteousness and purify my heart, O God.

Lord, I repent for any spiritual adultery or defilement in my life. Help me to turn away from all idolatry and false gods. Fill me with a genuine desire to seek You wholeheartedly and to know You more intimately.

Father, I surrender my pride and arrogance before You. I acknowledge that apart from You, I can do nothing. Help me to humble myself under Your mighty hand, that You may lift me up in due time.

Father, I intercede for those who are oppressed and broken in judgment. Bring healing and restoration to the brokenhearted, and may Your justice prevail in every situation. Show Your mercy and grace to those in need.

Heavenly Father, I acknowledge that You alone are my healer and deliverer. I renounce all reliance on human strength or worldly solutions. May I trust in You alone for my healing and restoration.

Father, I pray for a spirit of repentance and humility to sweep across the land. May Your people turn from their wicked ways and seek Your face earnestly. Show us Your mercy and forgiveness, O Lord.

Lord, I commit myself afresh to seek Your face and to acknowledge my need for You. May Your presence be my greatest desire and Your will my highest pursuit. In the name of Jesus, I surrender all to You.

Lord, I repent for the times when I have refused to return to You and have instead chosen to rely on my own strength and wisdom. Forgive me for my disobedience and rebellion. Draw me back to Yourself, O Lord.

Lord, I surrender my heart to You completely. Help me to exalt You and give You the highest place in my life. May my heart be steadfast in following after You, and may I never turn back from Your ways.

Father, empower me to walk in obedience to Your word and to follow after You wholeheartedly. Let Your presence go before me like a roaring lion, filling me with awe and reverence for Your majesty and power.

Lord, I trust in Your promises to restore and redeem me. Like a bird returning to its nest, I surrender myself to Your care and protection. Lead me into the fullness of Your blessings and establish me in Your perfect will.

Heavenly Father, cleanse me from all falsehood and deceit. Help me to walk in truth and integrity, honoring You in all aspects of my life. May I be faithful to You and live in accordance with Your word.

Lord, I surrender myself to Your nurturing presence, likened unto the dew upon Israel. May I grow and flourish in Your care, like a lily spreading its roots deep into the soil of Your love.

Father, I ask for angelic assistance and heavenly reinforcements to surround me and protect me from all harm. Let Your angels encamp around me, shielding me from every attack of the enemy.

Lord, I declare victory over every battle and every trial that I face. I am more than a conqueror through Christ who strengthens me. No weapon formed against me shall prosper, and every tongue that rises against me in judgment shall be condemned.

Heavenly Father, I resist the devil and his schemes in the mighty name of Jesus. I declare that no weapon formed against me shall prosper, and every tongue that rises against me in judgment shall be condemned.

Father, I plead the blood of Jesus over every area of my life that has been affected by spiritual bondage and darkness. I ask for

Your cleansing and protection, covering every aspect of my being.

Lord, I break every generational curse and stronghold that has been passed down through my family line. By the authority of Jesus Christ, I command every chain of bondage to be broken, and every yoke of oppression to be shattered.

Heavenly Father, I declare that I am chosen and beloved in Your sight. I reject every lie and accusation of the enemy, and I embrace the truth of Your Word that declares me as Your child, redeemed and set free.

Lord, I resist the spirit of Jezreel, which seeks to bring destruction and judgment upon my life. I take authority over every attack of the enemy and declare that no weapon formed against me shall prosper.

Lord, I declare victory over every spiritual battle and assignment that the enemy has waged against me. I stand firm in faith, knowing that You are fighting on my behalf, and that no enemy can stand against Your mighty power.

Father, I ask for Your forgiveness and cleansing from all sin and unrighteousness. I invite Your Holy Spirit to search my heart and reveal any hidden areas that need to be surrendered to You. In the name of Jesus, I break every chain of bondage and declare my freedom in Christ.

Lord, I ask for Your strength and courage to resist temptation and overcome every spiritual attack. Help me to walk in obedience and righteousness, relying on Your grace and power to sustain me. In the name of Jesus, I command every demonic stronghold to be demolished, and every captive to be set free.

I declare victory over every spirit of spiritual adultery and idolatry in my life. By the power of the Lord, I break free from every bondage to other gods and worldly pleasures that seek to draw me away from the true God.

In the name of Jesus, I proclaim my redemption and restoration from every form of captivity. I am bought with a price, redeemed by the precious blood of Jesus Christ. I declare my allegiance to the Lord and renounce all ties with the enemy.

By the authority of Jesus Christ, I declare that I abide in the love and faithfulness of the Lord. I reject every temptation to stray from His path and remain steadfast in His covenant. I declare that my heart is fixed on the Lord, and I will not be swayed by the enticements of the enemy.

I declare the breaking of every stronghold and bondage that has kept me in spiritual barrenness and desolation. In the name of Jesus, I command every obstacle to my spiritual growth and progress to be removed. I declare that I am free to walk in the fullness of God's promises and blessings.

I declare the fulfillment of God's promises of restoration and return in my life. By the power of the Holy Spirit, I seek the Lord wholeheartedly and fear Him with reverence and awe. I declare that I am walking in the abundance of God's goodness and mercy, and His kingdom is established in my heart and life.

In the name of Jesus, I declare freedom from the chains of sin that have entangled me. By the power of the blood of Christ, I break every stronghold and bondage in my life.

I proclaim victory over the lusts of the flesh, the lust of the eyes, and the pride of life. Sin shall no longer have dominion over me, for I am crucified with Christ.

In the name of Jesus, I break every generational curse and pattern of sin that has plagued my family line. I stand as a blood-bought child of God, liberated from the sins of my ancestors.

I decree the dismantling of every stronghold of addiction, whether it be to substances, behaviors, or thoughts. I am liberated by the transforming power of the Holy Spirit.

I declare that the power of sin is broken over my mind, my emotions, and my will. I am empowered by the Holy Spirit to resist temptation and walk in righteousness.

I proclaim freedom from the spirit of fear, guilt, and condemnation. I am forgiven, justified, and righteous in Christ Jesus, and no accusation or condemnation can stand against me.

In the name of Jesus, I break the power of every lie, deception, and deceitful spirit that seeks to lead me astray. I walk in the light of God's truth, and the truth has set me free.

By the authority of Jesus Christ, I command every demonic assignment and attack against my soul to be nullified and rendered powerless. I am covered and protected by the blood of the Lamb.

I declare that I am more than a conqueror through Him who loved me, and nothing shall separate me from the love of God in Christ Jesus. I am victorious over sin and every spiritual adversary.

In the name of Jesus, I rebuke every spirit of temptation, lust, and perversion that seeks to ensnare my soul. I am empowered to resist the devil, and he flees from me.

By the authority of Jesus Christ, I command every demonic stronghold and foothold in my life to be demolished and destroyed. I am free to walk in the liberty of the sons and daughters of God.

By the authority of Jesus Christ, I break every generational curse that has been passed down through my family line. I declare freedom from the patterns of sin and bondage that have afflicted my ancestors.

In the name of Jesus, I nullify and cancel every legal right that the enemy has held over my life through generational curses. I am released from the grip of generational bondage.

I declare that the power of the cross of Christ breaks every curse and releases me into the blessings of Abraham. I am an heir of God's promises, not a victim of generational curses.

By the blood of Jesus, I break every cycle of poverty, divorce, sickness, addiction, and dysfunction that has plagued my family for generations. I am liberated to walk in God's abundance and wholeness.

I decree that the generational curses of rebellion, idolatry, and disobedience are broken off my life and my descendants. I am aligned with God's purposes and plans for my family's future.

In the name of Jesus, I reclaim my identity and destiny as a child of God, free from the limitations and bondages of generational curses. I am empowered to live victoriously in Christ.

I prophesy restoration and redemption over my family lineage. Through the power of Jesus Christ, I declare that generational curses are replaced with generational blessings, and God's glory will shine through our heritage.

In the name of Jesus, I renounce and break every generational curse of divorce and marital discord that has plagued my family lineage. I declare that the cycle of broken relationships ends with me, and I walk in God's plan for lasting unity and love in my family.

By the blood of Jesus, I dismantle and destroy every satanic altar erected against the sanctity of marriage and family in my bloodline. I nullify their evil influence and decree divine protection over my relationships.

I command every demonic stronghold associated with generational divorce and satanic altars to be demolished in the mighty name of Jesus. I release the power of God's Word to bring freedom and restoration.

I bind and cast out every spirit of division, strife, and discord operating in my family lineage. I release the spirit of unity, love, and forgiveness to reign supreme in our midst.

I break every covenant made with demonic forces through ancestral participation in satanic rituals or occult practices. I declare my allegiance to Jesus Christ alone and renounce any ties to darkness.

I release the power of God's Word to bring healing and reconciliation to every broken relationship within my family. I declare that what the enemy meant for harm, God will turn around for good.

I declare that my family is a stronghold of God's love, peace, and unity. No curse or demonic assignment can prevail against the authority of Jesus Christ operating in our lives. We stand firm in faith, trusting in God's power to overcome every obstacle.

By the blood of Jesus, I dismantle and destroy every satanic altar erected to perpetuate stagnancy and lack in my family bloodline. I command every demonic force hindering progress to be scattered and rendered powerless.

I declare that my family is released from the grip of generational stagnancy, and we walk in the fullness of God's promises for prosperity, growth, and advancement in every area of our lives.

I bind and rebuke every spirit of delay, setback, and hindrance that operates through generational curses and satanic altars in my family. I release the spirit of acceleration and breakthrough into our midst.

I renounce and reject every evil covenant made with satanic forces through ancestral participation in occult practices or idol worship. I declare my allegiance to Jesus Christ alone, and His victory is our inheritance.

I declare that my family is breaking free from every generational curse and stronghold of stagnancy. We are stepping into a season of divine acceleration, where God's blessings overtake us and His favor opens doors of opportunity.

I speak life, abundance, and fruitfulness into every area of my family's life. I declare that we are rising above every obstacle and limitation, walking in the fullness of God's purpose and destiny for our lives.

I command every demonic assignment of failure and setback against my family to be nullified and destroyed. I release the angels of God to wage war on our behalf and to ensure our victory in every battle.

I uproot every seed of failure planted by the enemy in our minds and hearts. I declare that we are walking in the mind of Christ, filled with wisdom, courage, and faith to overcome every obstacle.

I prophesy success, prosperity, and divine favor over my family. I decree that doors of opportunity are opening, and every setback is turning into a setup for a miraculous breakthrough.

In the name of Jesus, I break every curse of financial instability and lack that has hindered my family's prosperity. I declare that we are heirs to the abundance of God's kingdom, and we walk in financial freedom and stability.

I rebuke every spirit of poverty, debt, and lack that has plagued my family for generations. By the authority of Jesus Christ, I command every hindrance to our financial stability to be removed, and I speak forth divine provision and abundance into our lives.

I decree and declare that our God is Jehovah Jireh, our provider. I trust in His promises to supply all our needs according to His riches in glory. I reject the lies of the enemy that seek to keep us bound in financial struggle, and I claim the blessings of prosperity and abundance over my family.

I cancel every negative word spoken against our financial stability and success. I declare that we are blessed coming in and blessed going out, and every area of our finances is prospering under the favor and grace of God.

I release a supernatural shift in our financial situation. I command doors of opportunity to open, divine connections to be made, and resources to flow abundantly into our lives. I declare that we are walking in the overflow, and our financial stability is a testimony to the faithfulness of our God.

I rebuke every spirit of barrenness and unfruitfulness operating in my life and family. By the power of the Holy Spirit, I command every hindrance to fertility and reproduction to be removed, and I speak forth divine fruitfulness and multiplication over us.

I declare that my body is a temple of the Holy Spirit, and it is blessed to conceive and bear children. I reject any medical diagnosis or prognosis that contradicts God's promise of fruitfulness in my life.

I stand on the word of God that says, "Be fruitful and multiply." I declare that the curse of barrenness is broken, and we shall experience the joy of parenthood and the blessing of children in our family.

Heavenly Father, I thank You for the talents and abilities You have blessed me with. I declare that every obstacle hindering my career advancement is removed in the mighty name of Jesus, and I step into new levels of success and prosperity.

I bind and rebuke every spirit of stagnation, limitation, and setback in my career path. I release the favor of God upon my professional endeavors, opening doors of promotion, opportunity, and advancement that no man can shut.

I pray for divine wisdom, insight, and discernment in my career decisions. May the Holy Spirit guide me in the right direction, leading me to opportunities that align with Your perfect will for my life and contribute to my advancement and growth.

I reject every negative word spoken against my career progression and success. I declare that I am destined for greatness, and I walk in the confidence that God's plans for me are of good and not of evil, to give me a future and a hope.

I decree and declare that I am the head and not the tail, above and not beneath. I break every curse of mediocrity and underachievement over my life and career, and I step into the fullness of God's purpose and abundance in my professional life.

I rebuke every spirit of confusion, distraction, and discouragement that seeks to hinder my learning and understanding. I declare clarity of mind, focus, and diligence in my studies, leading to excellence and success in every endeavor.

I pray for divine favor with my teachers, professors, and mentors. May they recognize and appreciate my efforts, granting me favor in their sight and opening doors of opportunity for academic advancement and achievement.

I reject every negative thought or belief that suggests failure or inadequacy in my academic pursuits. I declare that I am more than a conqueror through Christ who strengthens me, and I am destined for greatness in my educational journey.

I decree and declare that I am a vessel of God's wisdom and knowledge. I have the ability to grasp and retain information easily, to excel in exams and assessments, and to fulfill my academic goals with excellence, to the glory of God.

In the name of Jesus, I break every chain of marital delay that has bound my life and destiny. I command every hindering force to release its grip over my marital breakthrough now!

I reject and renounce every curse of marital delay spoken over my life and bloodline. By the power of the blood of Jesus, I am set free from all generational curses affecting my marital destiny.

I come against every spiritual force orchestrating delays in my marital journey. I declare that my time of divine connection and union is now, and no demonic agenda can hinder it.

I release the fire of God to consume every satanic altar erected to delay my marital blessings. Let every demonic stronghold hindering my marriage be demolished by the power of God!

I decree and declare that I am not meant to walk the path of loneliness and delay. I am destined for a blissful and timely marriage ordained by God, and I claim it by faith in Jesus' name.

I rebuke every spirit of fear, doubt, and insecurity that arises due to prolonged waiting for marriage. I receive the peace of God that surpasses all understanding, trusting in His perfect timing for my life.

I uproot every negative seed planted in my mind concerning marriage. I replace them with the promises of God for a fulfilling and timely marital union, according to His Word.

I pray for divine alignment with my future spouse. May God orchestrate our paths to intersect at the appointed time, leading to a blessed and fruitful marriage that glorifies His name.

I declare that my marital breakthrough is imminent. I refuse to lose hope or grow weary in waiting, for God's timing is perfect, and He will fulfill His promises concerning my marital destiny.

I seal these declarations with the authority of Jesus Christ, believing and receiving my marital breakthrough with unwavering faith. Let every delay be turned into acceleration, and let my testimony manifest for the glory of God!

-Amen

www.ingramcontent.com/pod-product-compliance
Lightning Source LLC
LaVergne TN
LVHW051129080426
835510LV00018B/2311